THE FILMS OF
AL PACINO

THE FILMS OF
AL PACINO

WILLIAM SCHOELL

A CITADEL PRESS BOOK
Published by Carol Publishing Group

A Citadel Press Book
Published by Carol Publishing Group
Citadel Press is a registered trademark of Carol Communications,
Inc.
Editorial Offices: 600 Madison Avenue, New York, N.Y. 10022
Sales and Distribution Offices: 120 Enterprise Avenue, Secaucus,
N.J. 07094
In Canada: Canadian Manda Group, One Atlantic Avenue,
Suite 105, Toronto, Ontario M6K 3E7
Queries regarding rights and permissions should be addressed to
Carol Publishing Group, 600 Madison Avenue, New York, N.Y.
10022

Carol Publishing Group books are available at special discounts
for bulk purchases, sales promotions, fund raising, or
educational purposes. Special editions can be created to
specifications. For details, contact Special Sales Department,
Carol Publishing Group, 120 Enterprise Avenue, Secaucus, N.J.
07094

Designed by A. Christopher Simon

Manufactured in the United States of America

10 9 8 7 6 5 4 3 2 1

LIBRARY OF CONGRESS CATALOGING-IN-PUBLICATION DATA

Schoell, William.
    The films of Al Pacino / by William Schoell.
        p.   cm.
    "A Citadel Press book."
    ISBN 0-8065-1596-1 (pbk.)
    1. Pacino, Al, 1940– —Criticism and interpretation.   I. Title.
PN2287.P18S36   1995   94-45535
791.43′028′092—dc20   CIP

Pacino at the height of his fame.

ACKNOWLEDGMENTS

The author tenders his appreciation to:
Allan J. Wilson, Lawrence J. Quirk, Gene Massimo, John Cocchi, Robert Heide, John Gilman, Billy Otis, Gregory Speck, Caroline Schoell, Arthur Tower, Jerry Ohlinger's Movie Material Store, the staff of the Billy Rose Theatre Collection at Lincoln Center, Howard Mandelbaum, Ron Mandelbaum, Ed Maguire of Photofest, Frank Lavena, and Margaret Wolf.
And to:
National General Pictures, Cinema Center Films, Dunne-Didion-Dunne Productions, 20th Century-Fox, Paramount, Warner Brothers, Dino De Laurentiis Productions, Columbia Pictures, Lorimar, Universal, Goldcrest Pictures, Viking Pictures, Touchstone, Silver Screen Partners IV, New Line Cinema, City Light Films, Epic Productions, Showtime, Albert S. Ruddy Productions, Francis Ford Coppola Productions, NBC-TV, Artists Entertainment Complex, Inc., United Artists, Jerry Weintraub Productions, Martin Bregman Productions, USA Network, Buena Vista Productions.

All of the stills in this book are from private collections.

CONTENTS

PART ONE
HIS LIFE

Portrait of an artist: Al Pacino.

Al Pacino may have "gone Hollywood," but he's a New York actor in every sense of the expression. First, he was born in New York City. Second, he got his early training in small theater companies in Manhattan and continues to tread the boards of both Broadway and off-Broadway theaters to this day. Third, fully half of his motion pictures take place almost entirely in New York City, and several others contain key sequences or large sections that take place in the area. Finally, there's something about the man—on the screen and off—that *screams* New York. You can see it in his performances (except when he's playing Cubans, maybe). Pacino has confessed that he loves the city; in many ways he *is* New York. He even plays the mayor in *City Hall*.

Pacino's early life was not exactly a New York success story, however. He was born Alfred Pacino on April 25, 1940, in East Harlem, to Rose and Salvatore Pacino. When Alfred was two, his father walked out on his mother, leaving Rose to fend for both herself and a young boy. Since she was unable to look after Al while she was working, she thought it would be best if he lived with her parents, James and Kate Gerard. Rose eventually moved in with them herself, only adding to the overcrowding in the Bronx tenement. Pacino spent his formative years living in cramped poverty.

Pacino's mother and grandparents were overprotective, so that the boy was rarely allowed outside until it was time for him to start school. For a time he found himself unable to cope and was victimized by both male and female bullies. He later learned to disarm them by telling them elaborate, made-up stories or enacting scenes from the many motion pictures his mother had taken him to see. He also delighted in acting out scenes for members of his family, who were charmed but who had no idea what it would lead to.

Becoming a class cutup did much for his popularity at school but little for his grades. The only activity he excelled at was performing in the student plays the class put on. By the time he was in the eighth grade he was showing such promise that his drama teacher made note of it in a letter to his mother. Rose saw this as a way for her "Sonny" to be somebody, and she echoed the teacher's suggestion that Al apply for admission to Manhattan's famous High School of Performing Arts.

Al's bid was successful, and he stayed at the school for two years. But several factors led to his becoming a dropout at age sixteen. To him, the whole Stanislavsky Method taught in the acting classes took all the fun out of acting, and he was failing in virtually every other subject. It was also a question of necessity. "My grandfather had retired, we had no money, and I was the sole support of my mother, who became ill," he told *New York Daily News* writer Glenn Plaskin. "She was a very high-strung and sensitive woman, an emotional person. . . . That's where I think I get some of my emotions."

His mother's "emotions" eventually drove him to

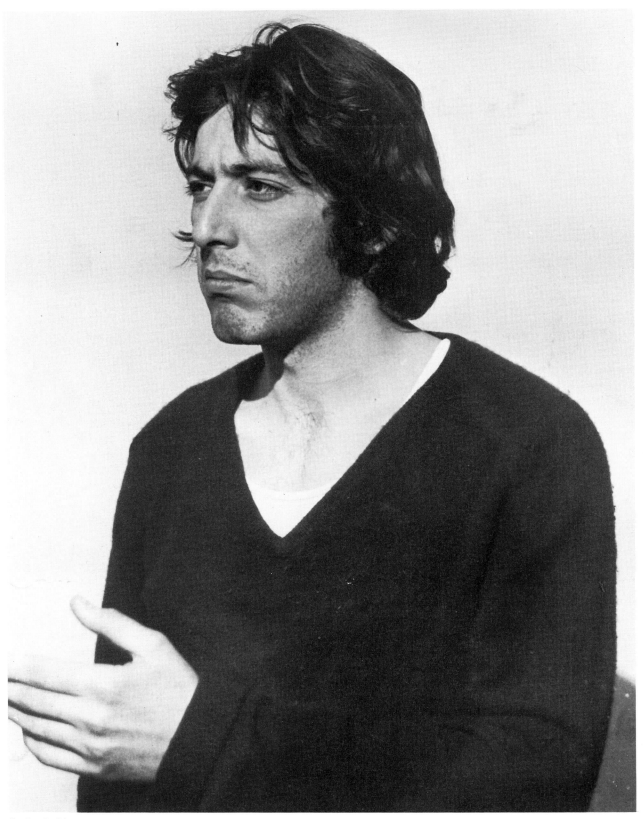

Pacino in his grungy prestardom period.

16

move to his own apartment; she had initially encouraged Sonny in his acting aspirations, but now she didn't think people from his lowly background could ever make it in show business. Hoping to prove her wrong, Al got a series of jobs to pay his rent (he would also send money home to his mother) and saved up for acting classes. He ushered at the Paris movie theater, delivered mail to the editorial staff of *Commentary,* and fixed leaky faucets as an apartment-house super.

At nineteen, Pacino moved to Greenwich Village, and it was there that his life as an artist truly began. A bright spot was his taking classes at the Herbert Berghof Studio, where he met twenty-nine-year-old acting coach Charlie Laughton and Laughton's actress-wife, Penny Allen, becoming close friends with both. Laughton was not only Pacino's coach but his confidant and older brother. The couple even fed Pacino on occasion, in addition to giving him tips on part-time jobs and acting auditions.

The next few years were creatively interesting but extremely difficult for Pacino. A big blow came when Al was twenty-two and his mother passed away unexpectedly. To this day he has trouble talking about it, some say because he was so immersed in his own problems at the time of her illness that he couldn't worry or even think about what she was going through. And, of course, there's the pain of knowing that his mother never lived to see what a success he would become. To make things worse, his grandfather died of cancer a year later.

"For me, losing them was devastating . . . a disaster that floored me," he said years later. "It was hard for me. . . . I always remember . . . and I miss, I miss my mother. They were the closest people to me, and I was not functioning very well. Later, I did therapy, but it was my friends in the theater that saved me."

On the professional front, Pacino tried to become a comedian, understudied for onetime roommate Martin Sheen in a "back alley" production, and worked as a stagehand for Julian Beck's Living Theater. On the personal front, he sank deeper and deeper into depression not only because of the deaths of mother and grandfather but because of what little headway he was making as an actor. He had to cadge money from friends, sneak meals where he could, find a bed to sleep in. Temporary jobs, such as moving furniture and passing out fliers on street corners, could only provide so much. Things got so bad emotionally that

he was counseled by one person to have himself committed!

Instead, he hung in there, eventually joining up with Joe Cino's Caffe Cino on Cornelia Street, which was also a hangout for such theatrical types as playwrights Sam Shepard, Lanford Wilson, and Robert Heide. Says Heide, "Pacino would do Shakespearean monologues. Joe Cino fed him—provolone and cappuccino." Cino, who later committed suicide, was a figurative godfather to many starving actors and writers. Cino did more than feed Pacino; he put on a production of William Saroyan's *Hello, Out There,* which was an outgrowth of one of Pacino's acting classes with Charlie Laughton. This led to other off-Broadway roles, an Obie nomination, and admission to the prestigious Actors Studio, run by famed acting coach Lee Strasberg.

Pacino was initially intimidated by the high-powered atmosphere at the Studio. "He was always in the shadows, sitting by himself," says Robert Heide, "with this kind of surly attitude." Later, Pacino became friends with—and won the respect of—Strasberg. Like Laughton and Allen, Strasberg gave Pacino lots of encouragement, along with the occasional handout. Pacino never forgot his early roots or the small kindnesses. Says Billy Otis, an actor who studied with Pacino and Laughton, "Al is a very loyal friend; his relationship with Charlie Laughton proves that." Pacino paid tribute to Laughton when he won his Oscar for *Scent of a Woman.* And he remains "very supportive of small theater," says Otis. Pacino doesn't forget the people who've helped him.

In the late sixties things started coming together for Pacino. First, he won an Obie for Best Actor in the 1967–68 production of *The Indian Wants the Bronx* by Israel Horovitz. Then he debuted on Broadway in Don Petersen's *Does a Tiger Wear a Necktie?* and won a Tony for Best Supporting Actor. His film debut came in 1969, when he had a bit—but a memorable one—in the Patty Duke starrer *Me, Natalie.* From the very first he exuded potent authority and charisma.

At the age of twenty-nine Pacino stood five feet seven inches tall and weighed approximately 165 pounds, a figure that might fluctuate now and then but which remained pretty constant over the years. Pacino kept himself in good shape. Some people thought that his comparative shortness might prevent him from making it to the top, but they couldn't have been more wrong. Another person who had faith in him was Martin Bregman, an entertainment manager who signed him after seeing him in *The Indian Wants the Bronx.*

Bregman's clients included Faye Dunaway and her boyfriend, Jerry Schatzberg, who was about to direct his second picture, *The Panic in Needle Park* (1971). Through these connections, Pacino found himself in the lead, with Kitty Winn as his costar. The film was a very graphic, frank study of degenerating heroin addicts, and both actors threw themselves into their research. Preparing for their roles, they could often be found talking to addicts and dealers who hung out in "Needle Park" on Manhattan's West Seventy-second Street. Pacino already had firsthand knowledge of the negative, indeed disastrous, effects of drug addiction: Two of his friends had overdosed and died. On another occasion he almost tripped over the body of a young actor he knew who had "OD'd" in an alleyway.

Pacino's performance in *The Panic in Needle Park* did not make him a star, but it did get him some serious attention from filmmakers. It also was the first time he unleashed his trademark "Pacino blast." An intense, moody, passionate actor—and person—to begin with, Pacino always pulls out all the stops in scenes when the character he's playing is supposed to get *mad.* Like a thespian equivalent of a fire-breathing dragon, Pacino uses voice, limbs, every part of him, to create a savage portrait of someone who is temporarily *out of control,* unstoppable, brutally larger than life, maniacally physical. This may or may not be "showy" acting, but it is *not* "overacting." Pacino's blasts always fit the character and the moment, and he uses them sparingly. Most (but not all) of his pictures have one, which Pacino's fans really look forward to.

Pacino got right into the big leagues with his next picture, *The Godfather* (1972), at thirty-two years of age. He received only $35,000 for several months of work and nearly didn't get the part; the studio was more interested in casting Warren Beatty, Robert Redford, Jack Nicholson, or even Frank Langella as Michael Corleone. Pacino didn't help matters by coming unprepared to his audition, doing ill-advised ad-libs, and moaning that he'd rather play the more violent, temperamental Sonny (James Caan). His behavior led initial booster Mario Puzo (who wrote the novel and cowrote the screenplay) to turn against him, with only director Francis Ford Coppola still in his corner. There were more auditions, more delays. Pacino wondered

if a big-time Hollywood adaptation of a best-selling novel was the right project for a "serious" actor, but he *wanted* the part. When he was finally offered the role for real, M-G-M promptly sued him because of a verbal agreement to appear in *The Gang That Couldn't Shoot Straight.* Bregman engineered a settlement.

Pacino was delighted to be working with idol Marlon Brando, old theatrical pal and former costar John Cazale (who was cast as Fredo Corleone), and Diane Keaton, with whom he entered into a long-term relationship, but otherwise he felt much like an outsider on *The Godfather* set. Although Pacino was really the

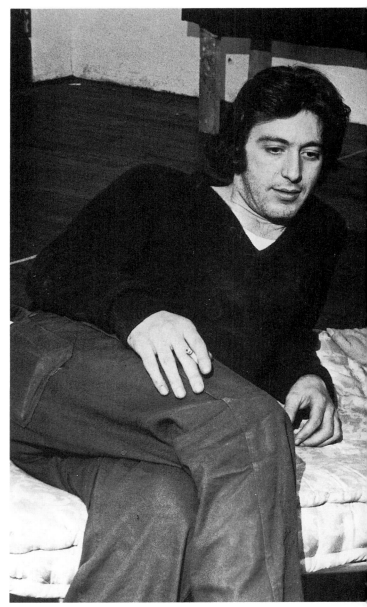

Pacino listens as a colleague instructs him in the early days.

main character and true star of the film, Brando received a Best Actor Oscar nomination and Pacino only a Best Supporting Actor nomination. Matters weren't helped when Bregman, his manager, issued the statement that "people may have come to see Brando, but they'll go away talking about Pacino." The statement was wrongly attributed to an "immodest" Pacino by the press, inciting Brando's ire: "I should have crushed the prick like a fly!" the portly "godfather" ranted, in character no doubt.

Despite his new fame, Pacino had no intention of forsaking the stage and appeared in David Rabe's

Basic Training of Pavlo Hummel as well as a risky production of Shakespeare's *Richard III*. His film career continued with *Scarecrow* (1973), helmed by *Panic in Needle Park*'s Jerry Schatzberg. Good friend Penny Allen was given a small part, and Gene Hackman was signed as costar. Hackman and Pacino had absolutely no rapport, and there were numerous off-screen altercations. The two would never work with each other again, not enemies but hardly friends.

Pacino's first big *solo* starring part was in *Serpico* (1973), playing a real-life cop who exposed corruption in the department and nearly paid for it with his life. Al and Frank Serpico, who had certain interests, such as opera, in common, got along famously, but such was not the case with producer Dino De Laurentiis and original director John G. Avildsen. The two had such operatic quarrels that they nearly tore the wallpaper off the boardroom in De Laurentiis's offices. Sidney Lumet was brought in as Avildsen's replacement, with felicitous results. Pacino's performance garnered a Best Actor nomination from the Academy, as did his next two pictures; alas, he was a three-time "loser." The consolation prize? *Serpico* turned Pacino into a major star. *The Godfather, Part II* (1974) and *Dog Day Afternoon* (1975) only entrenched him further in the firmament.

Proof of his stardom was his fee for *The Godfather, Part II:* $600,000, almost *twenty* times as much as he received for appearing in *The Godfather.* (He also got 10 percent of the sequel's profits.) Furthermore, he had enough clout to get friend and teacher Lee Strasberg his *very first* role in a motion picture, and for a better price than first offered. Lastly, he had developed that certain movie star "attitude."

Robert Heide, who had rented a 1954 Packard he co-owned with John Gilman to the producers of *The Godfather, Part II,* attended a boat party hosted by an Actors Studio associate around the time of the filming. According to Heide, Pacino, who was also there, "had an attitude. He wanted to be treated like a regular guy; on the other hand, if you didn't treat him like 'Al Pacino'—*fuck you*! It was clear that he had conflicted feelings."

To Pacino, all the attention and adulation were overwhelming; worse so if he had, as some have suggested, a shy streak. His way of dealing with it was to drink even more than usual. After a while it became a problem.

Pacino was no stranger to alcohol. He had begun

19

Pacino drops his grungy style for a sleeker look as he gets older.

to enjoy liquor and its uplifting properties in his early teens. In later years, alcohol would help him deal with his grief over family deaths and his career disappointments. Occasionally, he'd go on binges that would last for several days (although such self-destructive behavior was not a frequent occurrence). Alcohol would help him through difficult moments, such as watching himself for the first time in *The Panic in Needle Park* during its first public screening or attending a meeting with Bregman in which his manager extricated him from M-G-M's lawsuit over *The Gang That Couldn't Shoot Straight.* Liquor helped him relax; he could talk to people more easily with a few drinks in his system. Also, there was the simple fact that he *enjoyed*—as millions do—sitting in a barroom with friends and getting pleasantly looped.

But his good friend Charlie Laughton argued that Pacino was overdoing it; Pacino was drinking heavily night after night after night. Laughton felt that Pacino was an alcoholic and if he didn't stop drinking he would destroy everything it had taken him so long to achieve. It was quite some time before Pacino came to share this point of view. He attended a couple of AA meetings, which he found helpful, but basically cut out the drinking on his own. Whether Pacino was ever a bona fide *addict* of alcohol or just an immoderate partyer is debatable; in either case, the excessive consumption of alcohol would have played havoc with his health.

Pacino followed *The Godfather, Part II* with *Dog Day Afternoon,* in which he essayed a nebbish bank robber who has two wives, one of whom is a man. Pacino was the first major star to play "gay" in a popular film. Penny Allen appeared with him. Pacino was also instrumental in getting Julian Beck's (of the Living Theater) wife, Judith Molina, cast as his mother—Pacino never forgot those who were kind to him in the past. He got another Oscar nomination for his performance.

On-set battles between Pacino and director Sydney Pollack didn't help *Bobby Deerfield* (1977), his next film, one bit. Not only was Pacino not in tune with what Pollack was aiming for; Pollack lost patience with Pacino's deliberate acting style. The picture had to do with a racing driver's romance with a woman who was terminally ill, played by Marthe Keller. Ironically, Pacino's close friend John Cazale, with whom he had appeared onstage and in the *Godfather* films and *Dog Day Afternoon,* was diagnosed with incurable

bone cancer the year of *Bobby Deerfield's* release; he died the following March.

It was through costar Marthe Keller that Pacino finally got to meet his chief acting rival, Dustin Hoffman. The two had been carrying on a kind of mock press-fueled "feud" for years. Pacino and Hoffman had been aware of each other since their early days in the Actor's Studio, where each was serenaded with lavish descriptions of the other's brilliance. In 1966, Pacino was nominated for an Obie, but Hoffman walked off with the prize. After Hoffman's *Graduate* opened in 1967 (four whole years before Pacino's first *starring* film role in *The Panic in Needle Park*), Pacino not only had to put up with tales of Hoffman's big success, he even found himself being confused with his fellow actor on certain occasions. Since Pacino is a much sexier and better-looking man—and a very different type of actor—than the rather rodential (if talented) Hoffman, these occasions could not have much endeared his rival to him. Their compact figures are about all they have in common.

Yet reviewers continued to make comparisons. Pacino was accused of doing a takeoff on Hoffman's "Ratso Rizzo" of *Midnight Cowboy* in his own *Panic in Needle Park,* even though the films were made concurrently. *New Yorker* critic Pauline Kael— in one phase of her campaign to seemingly discredit herself with bird-brained, ill-conceived opinions—declared that Hoffman and Pacino were "indistinguishable" from one another. Now and then the two actors were up for the same roles, although this happened far less often than one would imagine. They are simply not the same type at all. According to Pacino's biographer Andrew Yule, Hoffman, for his part, jokingly refers to Pacino as his "nemesis."

Keller, who had worked with Hoffman in *Marathon Man,* brought him along for her first meeting with Pacino (on the eve of filming *Bobby Deerfield*) at Hoffman's request. Reports vary, with some saying it was hate at first sight between the two men and others insisting that it was a perfectly cordial meeting but that Pacino and Hoffman would never be good friends; they were different kinds of people as well as actors. One thing is for certain: It was not "hate at first sight" as far as Pacino and Keller were concerned; the two became lovers.

For a while there was little love lost between Pacino and one of his prime patrons, manager Martin Bregman. Bregman was tired of the managerial game and

It's back to "grunge," but only for a role. *Serpico* put Pacino into the front rank of Hollywood actors.

the pressures and demands of clients and decided to turn producer, with his top choice the story of Vietnam vet Ron Kovic, *Born on the Fourth of July.* Pacino was strongly interested in the role and got to know Kovic very well in preparation but bailed out when there was trouble with financing and in determining the right director. Everyone has a different story about who was ultimately to blame for the Pacino version's not getting made (it was later filmed with Tom Cruise in the lead), but the upshot was that Bregman produced no Pacino films for several years and for some time Oliver Stone dished Pacino all over town. Some feel that without Bregman's guidance, Pacino made a couple of bad choices when it came to future film projects.

Although its box office may not have been "boffo," *. . . and Justice for All* (1979) could not have been called a "bad choice"; Pacino was again nominated for a Best Actor Oscar for his performance as a Baltimore lawyer. His next picture, however, was another matter: *Cruising* (1980) may have been an entertaining thriller, but it did little business despite all the press it got due to its controversial nature. Director William Friedkin and company felt that a series of recent real-life murders in Greenwich Village's gay community (which was what the film was about) meant that their movie was too topical to be ignored; they were wrong. Everyone ignored it except for extremely vocal gay-activist protesters, who picketed the location filming. *Cruising* came out years too early to take advantage of the current "serial killer" craze. (Ironically, as of this writing, a new real-life serial killer has claimed the lives of several gay men in New York in the nineties and has still not been apprehended.)

Serpico: Pacino as a cop whose associates are mostly corrupt.

Pacino also made an unfortunate choice with *Author! Author!* (1982), in which he played a playwright with a runaway wife, a son, and several stepchildren. He presumably took the part because the screenplay was written by Israel Horovitz; Pacino had appeared in his stage work *The Indian Wants the Bronx* some years before. Director Arthur Hiller had several on-set blowups with Pacino, and most agree the film did little to take advantage of Pacino's particular abilities.

Pacino continued to "tread the boards," appearing in such plays as *American Buffalo* by David Mamet, *The Resistible Rise of Arturo Ui* by Bertolt Brecht, and a new production of *The Basic Training of Pavlo Hummel,* for which he won a Tony, among others. By 1983 he was back with Martin Bregman and into more appropriate film fare, *Scarface,* essaying a Cuban drug dealer on his way to the top in Miami. To many fans, Pacino's "Tony Montana" is his most flamboyant role and zestily sensational performance. He and the film got mixed notices, however. Again, one of his films

Pacino unveils a new hairstyle for *Dog Day Afternoon.*

was steeped in controversy, with Cuban-American protesters complaining that *Scarface* did for them what *Cruising* did for gays; that is, nothing (except stereotype them). Fear of militant activity led the production to move from Miami to a less volatile (at that time) Los Angeles.

Al Pacino is rare for a movie star. Instead of sticking to safe commercial ventures, he also needs to do the occasional work of art. This is proven not only by his continued interest in the theater (including Shakespeare!) but his willingness to do projects like the long-shot production of Hugh Hudson's *Revolution* (1985) and his own film version of Heathcote Williams's *Local Stigmatic.* The latter was originally staged at the Actors Playhouse in 1969 (see play section). Intrigued by the story line, Pacino spent hundreds of thousands of dollars of his own money shooting the film (it was directed by David Wheeler) and perpetually reediting it until a fifty-minute rough cut was available for limited screenings.

"I only made it because I wasn't finished with my character," Pacino told one interviewer. "Maybe that's why I'm still working. You have no way of getting to know a character immediately. He'll pop up, but it takes time. You've got to get a sense of the ambience." In any case, *The Local Stigmatic* remains an unfinished film and in all likelihood will never be released theatrically or shown at anything but special screenings.

As for *Revolution,* the ambitious and interesting film

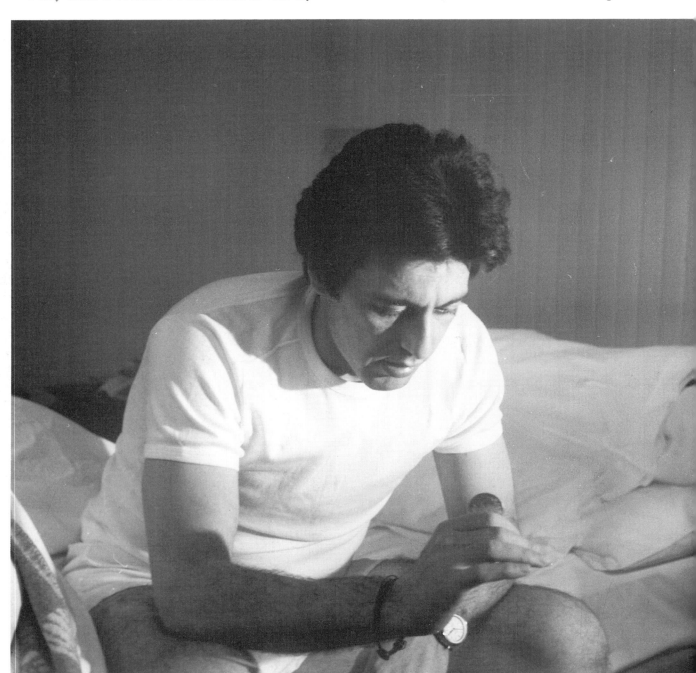

Pacino meditates over a role in the 1970s.

24

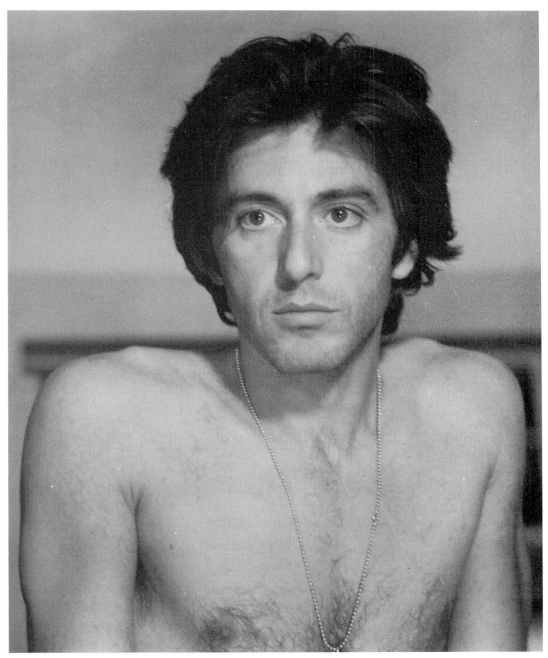

A skinny Pacino in the late-1970s period.

was deemed a financial and critical failure despite all the hard work and good intentions and its noble attempt to do something "different" (by 1985 standards, at least). Undoubtedly, its failure was a major disappointment to Pacino and Hudson both. Pacino did not make another movie for four years. His last *solid* hit had been *Dog Day Afternoon* ten years before.

Pacino's "comeback" film was *Sea of Love* (1989), coproduced by Martin Bregman, which made money

An intense Pacino as a racing-car driver in 1977's *Bobby Deerfield*.

and garnered raves for Pacino. He was back on top again, and a variety of interesting offers came his way. He was nominated (again!) for Best Supporting Actor for his exemplary work in Warren Beatty's *Dick Tracy* (1990). The charming film got mixed reviews from the critics; Hollywood insiders were more interested in which swinging bachelor would get to first base with sexy costar Madonna—Beatty or Pacino? Pacino may have had his way with the women, but it was Beatty who was spotted more than once strutting from Madonna's dressing room smeared with her trademark crimson lipstick.

By 1990 and the time of *The Godfather, Part III*, friends and associates of Pacino were wondering if he would finally marry Diane Keaton, with whom he had had a relationship as on-again, off-again as Michael Corleone's with wife Kay. But by 1990 Pacino had had relationships with *many* women, including some of his costars. Pacino has never lacked for female companionship and has had innumerable long-term relationships that never quite made it to the altar.

Reportedly, Pacino had his first girlfriend at age sixteen, when he dropped out of the High School of Performing Arts in order to make money for his family. He moved into his own apartment and shacked up with the young lady. If he had to give up some dreams and toil at tedious employment so soon in life, at least he had the compensations of his own place and a gal to go with it. There have also been many rumors about how Pacino managed to get by between acting gigs and part-time employment in the days before stardom. On at least one occasion, he went home with an older lady who offered him bed and board in exchange for sex. Pacino wouldn't have been the first actor to hustle for some extra dough.

Actress Susan Tyrrell (*Fat City*), a buxom, blowsy brunet who appeared in some plays with Pacino, was one of his earlier theatrical conquests. Another was Jill Clayburgh (*An Unmarried Woman*), whom he met while appearing at the Charles Playhouse in Boston. Pacino was Clayburgh's first-ever boyfriend, and her womanly instincts were aroused enough by his ministrations for her to follow him back to New York and move into a fifth-floor walk-up with him. Clayburgh stayed with Pacino during his worst periods of heavy drinking and on top of that had to watch him become a star in *The Godfather* while her career limped along until *An Unmarried Woman* in 1978. Clayburgh definitely drew on much of her five-year experience with Pacino for her performance in the picture, but she would have remained an "unmarried woman" had she stayed with him. The two broke up in 1972. Years later, Clayburgh married playwright David Rabe, in whose work Pacino appeared. Pacino loved Clayburgh but wasn't ready for marriage.

Next came a brief dalliance with Tuesday Weld (*Pretty Poison*), who had been a hot tamale in her teens, outdrinking and outsexing even Pacino. By 1972 she was coming out of a failed marriage to a writer who had probably gotten blisters on his typing fingers trying to tame her. The "wilder" Pacino was more Weld's speed, but only until she could land the diminutive comedian Dudley Moore, whom she married. This union didn't last very long, either, but at least Pacino was spared the mistake of marrying the tempestuous Tuesday. Ten years later, Pacino found himself *playing* Tuesday's husband in *Author! Author!*;

although Weld was cast, amusingly enough, as a "wild" wife, her appearance had become comparatively matronly by then.

Diane Keaton's relationship with Pacino—she met him on the set of *The Godfather*—spanned all three Mafia miniepics and nearly two decades. For a long time she was the lady love of fellow Hollywood cocksman Warren Beatty, and she also dallied with Woody Allen in pre-Mia days. By the late 1980s Keaton was back with Pacino, probably because Beatty was too *much* the tomcat and Woody Allen a distant third to begin with. She and Pacino shared a villa in Rome during the filming of *The Godfather, Part III*, but as the weeks progressed, things became strained. Reportedly, Keaton had already miscarried Pacino's baby; she not only wanted another child but marriage and stability. Pacino could offer neither, and the relationship was over.

One of Pacino's most "serious" lovers was Marthe Keller, with whom he costarred in *Bobby Deerfield*. Their relationship, oddly, somewhat mirrored the one in the film, with Keller more free spirited and demonstrative and Pacino more cautious and laid back. After filming, Keller moved into his apartment and got him to change his style of dress. A minor health problem of Keller's, before diagnosis, made them wonder if life was going to imitate art (Keller dies in *Bobby Deerfield*) and spell finis to their relationship. Instead, it died of natural causes. Pacino was in love with Keller, but not quite ready to commit himself fully to her.

This was evidenced by the presence of young actress Maureen Springer in his life, both personal and professional. Springer was given the part of his girlfriend in *Cruising*, but she was hastily replaced by Karen Allen when her affair with Pacino bit the dust. *She* was replaced in his affections by Kathleen Quinlan (*I Never Promised You a Rose Garden*), with whom he was heavily and very romantically involved in the early to mid-eighties. Although both spoke to friends in glowing terms of their love and high regard for each other, things had petered out by 1985, when Pacino would give a blast to anyone who even spoke of her.

After Quinlan, Pacino had a brief interlude with Jan Tarrant, who had been an acting teacher at the Strasberg Institute. He segued from Tarrant to Tarrant's "great friend" (according to one columnist) Annie Praeger. Things went hot and heavy with Ms. Praeger for a while, until Annie found out that Pacino had

Al Pacino on the town with his first *major* lady love, actress Jill Clayburgh.

had a love child with buddy Jan. When news of the child leaked out, Pacino's publicist, Pat Kingsley, did her best to downplay it, issuing a terse statement that Pacino "does have a daughter. I won't go further than that."

Later on, Pacino was only too happy to acknowledge his daughter by Tarrant, Julie Marie. "I love being a father, and I'm actively involved," he told Glenn Paskin. "What a *relief* to see that life is not about me; it's about *her*. I can be away from Julie for a certain time, but then I have a real *need* to see her that's beyond my control. Fatherhood has changed me in a big way—and in lots of little ways." One friend agreed: "It's a totally different Al."

Since Pacino was not romantically involved with Julie Marie's mother or with her friend Praeger, he was wide open to the advances of current (as of this writing) girlfriend Lyndall Hobbs, a (now) forty-one-year-old Australian director. As many columnists have gleefully noted, things have not always gone smoothly in the relationship between Pacino and Hobbs. Reportedly, Hobbs was not well liked by many of Pacino's friends and associates, especially because she was perceived as being too "controlling." In particular, tension exists between Hobbs and producer Martin Bregman, Pacino's former manager, reportedly because Bregman felt Pacino should have stayed with Hobbs's predecessor, Annie Praeger, while Hobbs thinks of Bregman as someone who is only out to use Al for his own purposes. Parts of an angry letter Hobbs sent Bregman surfaced on page 6 of the *New York Post*, but Bregman denied ever receiving it. As for Hobbs? "It's old news," she stated through her assistant.

Of more immediate concern to Hobbs were reports that Pacino was seeing Praeger again, not to mention his relationship with *Carlito's Way* costar Penelope Ann Miller. Pacino kept mum about the affair, which lasted for several months, but Ms. Miller was practically calling press conferences about it once it was over, ensuring several inches of press clippings. To her it was no "fling"; she was really in love, she said, although it had not been her intention that that should happen. For his part, Pacino stated about affairs with costars: "A lot of people think that it allows you to bring personal things to the work, but it isn't true. . . ."

Pacino and the second lady he was *really* in love with: actress Marthe Keller.

29

Pacino as the sinister Tony Montana of *Scarface*.

It's an interference." Miller consoled herself with handsome musician Gary Allegretto, while Pacino "returned" to Hobbs.

Not much later, Hobbs staged a reading of a screenplay she cowrote about a woman whose husband is cheating on her; a said-to-be "squirming" Pacino was in attendance. Pacino's attitude toward Hobbs: "They say whatever works for you, and she works for me."

Pacino may never get married—he feels he doesn't need that piece of paper—but whenever a relationship fails, he always has one faithful "spouse" waiting in the wings, the only love that truly matters: his work.

Pacino's hair was grayed for his role of an aging Michael Corleone in *The Godfather, Part III.*

Pacino as he is today.

For creative sustenance, there are his theatrical assignments. For money, there is the movies. Pacino was paid $6 million for *Frankie and Johnny* (1991), $1.5 million for a smaller role in *Glengarry Glen Ross* (1992) and another $6 million for *Carlito's Way* (1993). After *finally* winning an Oscar for his performance in *Scent of a Woman* (1992), his asking price will undoubtedly go up.

In February 1993, Pacino was honored with a tribute at the Waldorf-Astoria, hosted by the American Museum of the Moving Image (AMMI), partly because he had just been nominated for two Oscars in the same year (for *Glengarry* and *Scent of a Woman*). In her witty write-up in the New York *Post*, Jami Bernard said that the crowd at the event "was about as electrified as a beached whale." Bernard blamed neither Pacino nor the AMMI but all of the "listless" presenters. Bernard spoke for many when she wrote that his "is a rare talent. Pacino is so good he can now unbalance movies that aren't up to his speed." For a retrospective of his films at the AMMI's Astoria, Queens, headquarters, Pacino supervised the reediting of the master-piece-that-wasn't, *Revolution*. (Apparently this new version has never been released theatrically or on videocassette.)

Many interesting film projects await Pacino after *City Hall*, one or all of which may eventually materialize. These include a film version of David Mamet's *American Buffalo*, costarring Robert De Niro and Leonardo Di Caprio, directed by John McNaughton; a remake of *Love Me or Leave Me* with Winona Ryder as singer Ruth Etting (originally played by Doris Day in the 1955 version) and Pacino stepping into Jimmy Cagney's shoes as the gangster she's involved with, directed by Harold (*Sea of Love*) Becker; and an untitled crime thriller for Warner Brothers which would again team Pacino with Robert De Niro. Pacino had planned to do a bio of Manuel Noriega for Oliver Stone, but Stone canceled the production in early 1994.

Whatever Pacino decides upon, there is no doubt that he will be riveting audiences for many years to come.

PART TWO
HIS FILMS

James Farentino is Patty Duke's dream guy in *Me, Natalie*, but she'd probably have been happier with Pacino.

ME, NATALIE

A National General Pictures release; a Cinema Center Films presentation, 1969

Producer, Stanley Shapiro; director, Fred Coe; director of photography, Arthur J. Ornitz; editor, Sheila Bakerman; screenplay, A. Martin Zweiback; based on a story by Stanley Shapiro; associate producer, Kurt Newmann; music, Henry Mancini (with lyrics by Rod McKuen); art director, George Jenkins. Running time: 111 min.

CAST

Patty Duke (*Natalie Miller*); James Farentino (*David*); Nancy Marchand (*Mrs. Miller*); Martin Balsam (*Uncle Harold*); Elsa Lanchester (*Miss Dennison*); Salome Jens (*Shirley Norton*); Philip Sterling (*Mr. Miller*); Deborah Winters (*Betty Simon*); Ron Hale (*Stanley Dexter*); Bob Balaban (*Morris*); Al Pacino (*Tony*).

Al Pacino's screen debut was not especially auspicious, but he proved that he had *presence* right from the very start.

Me, Natalie was a Patty Duke project from the word go. The director, Fred Coe, had produced both the play and film versions of Duke's triumph *The Miracle Worker,* and this whole project was built around the talents of the former "Helen Keller." Pacino had only a bit part, as a tough guy named Tony.

Natalie Miller (Patty Duke) is a plain girl from Brooklyn who is tormented by her lack of beauty and the terrible blind dates that her well-meaning parents are always planning for her. She goes so far as to pretend that she has a date for the prom just so they won't set her up with anyone. Her uncle Harold (Martin Balsam), who always calls her his "little princess," assures her that substance is more important than beauty, but Natalie is completely disillusioned when she meets the woman he has chosen to marry: a blond go-go dancer and bimbo (Salome Jens). When Harry dies, she refuses to go to his funeral.

Eventually, Natalie winds up in the East Village, where she interacts with a kooky landlady (Elsa Lanchester), and a neighbor, David Harris (James Farentino), who was a successful architect now planning to become an artist. He asks Natalie to pose for him, and the two soon fall in love. When she learns that David is married, Natalie botches a suicide attempt by jumping in the East River during low tide! David assures her that he will divorce his wife and convinces her to move in with him. But while he's in Connecticut finalizing his affairs, Natalie changes her mind and realizes that she can't be responsible for the breakup of his marriage. Their affair has given her the confidence to go on alone. (Inexplicably, she moves back in with her parents!)

Pacino shows up about halfway through the picture, during a dance sequence that he spent a whole day shooting. He asks his partner if she "puts out." When she replies indignantly in the negative, he snaps, "Listen! Somebody like you oughta be asking *me!*" In his minute or so of screen time he gets across that prickly insolence and charisma that would become his trademark.

The film was shot all over New York City, which delighted producer Stanley Shapiro. "Every single foot of this film is being made in New York," he told reporters, "and the whole process has been a happy one. It's the most professional crew I have ever seen. The police have been fantastic. Even the people have been great. We had two thousand people standing there out in Brooklyn, and we told them to be quiet, and they were quiet."

The gritty *Me, Natalie* seemed a change of pace for Shapiro, who had formerly produced glossy Doris Day films like *Pillow Talk* and *Move Over, Darling*. Some critics quipped that with this picture he was still working with a "virgin."

Me, Natalie got very mixed reviews, with many critics suggesting that it was corny, sitcomish, contrived, and much too "cute" by far. Fred Coe's "mod" direction also came under attack. However, *Saturday Review* opined, "Natalie is . . . a creature of delightful wit and warmth—and so is the film which tells her story."

Donald J. Mayerson, in the *Villager*, felt just the opposite: "(Natalie) moves to Greenwich Village, meets two homosexuals, freaks out on LSD, falls in love with a married artist who deflowers her and finally discovers her identity, which is, by the way, hardly worth writing home about . . . the worst piece of publicity about Greenwich Village to come along since that psychotic Nazi in *The Producers*."

Mayerson did add, however, that "Al Pacino, in a bit part as an aggressive hood, is funny." Praising the performances (if not the picture) in *New York*, Judith Crist listed Al Pacino before the other supporting players (who had much bigger parts) and purred that they

Al Pacino had only a bit part in *Me, Natalie* as a hood named Tony.

Patty Duke has reason to smile. *She* was the star of *Me, Natalie*—Pacino's film debut—and not Pacino.

all "matched the perfection" of Duke and Balsam in the leads.

Bob Balaban, who played the nervous character who gives John Voight a blow job in a movie theater that same year in *Midnight Cowboy,* also got good notices in *Me, Natalie* as nerdy Morris, an acne-ridden optometrist who is rebuffed when Natalie tells him she's a call girl but who calls her later to say he's raised the money.

Outfitted with a fake putty nose and large buck teeth to make her homely, Patty Duke received generally good notices, although not everyone was taken by her performance, with one critic suggesting she was just walking through the picture without even acting.

One of the most admirable things about *Me, Nata-lie*—which is an uneven, often exasperating picture—is that it resists making Natalie herself too sweet or entirely likable, realizing that her torment would realistically turn her into someone who was not always pleasant or reasonable. The trouble with the movie is that it becomes pure Hollywood (despite those New York locations) wish fulfillment when the handsome artist "falls in love" with the abrasive, unattractive Duke. (We're never shown what it is he sees in her.) Worse, Duke dumps the artist for unselfish motives that are somewhat contrary to her character.

Despite excellent performances and some fine scenes, *Me, Natalie* smacks of compromise; a noble, ambitious attempt is muffed.

Pacino, at least, would go on to better things.

The Panic in Needle Park: Pacino's second picture—and his first starring role.

THE PANIC IN NEEDLE PARK

20th Century-Fox; a Dunne Didion Dunne production, 1971

Producer, Dominick Dunne; director, Jerry Schatzberg; director of photography, Adam Holender; editor, Evan Lottman; screenplay, Joan Didion and John Gregory Dunne; based on the book by James Mills; associate producer, Roger M. Rothstein; costume design, Jo Ynocencio; art director, Murray P. Stern. Running time: 110 min.

CAST

Al Pacino (*Bobby*); Kitty Winn (*Helen*); Richard Bright (*Hank*); Alan Vint (*Hotch*); Warren Finnerty (*Sammy*); Kiel Martin (*Chico*); Raul Julia (*Marco*); Paul Sorvino (*Samuels*); Dora Weissman (*Pawnshop Lady*); Bryant Fraser (*Prep-School Boy*).

Hangout of heroin addicts and dealers, Manhattan's Sherman Square (located at West Seventy-second Street where Broadway and Amsterdam Avenue intersect) had become known as "Needle Park" by the sixties. The "panic" of the title refers to what drug addicts feel when their supply has run out.

The Panic in Needle Park is a gritty study of the kind of people who have contributed more than their share

Kitty Winn was Pacino's "companion in nightmare" in *The Panic in Needle Park*.

The lost denizens of New York's "Needle Park," Bobby and Helen among them.

42

Helen (Kitty Winn) and Bobby (Al Pacino) enjoying a lazy afternoon.

to the decline of New York and all great cities in the United States: drug dealers and users. Made at the height of the hippie/love/drugs-are-great period in this country, *Panic* deserves high marks for having the courage to present the downside of indiscriminate drug use during a time when no one wanted to hear it. Admittedly, the characters in this movie are heavy into hard drugs, heroin—they are not casual joint smokers—but the movie had important points to make during a period when popular culture was doing its best to make drugs seem like the magic cure-all for every ailment that could befall one. This is not to say it was necessarily intended to be a "message" film; it gets its point across with a proliferation of documentary-like detail.

Bobby (Pacino) and Helen (Kitty Winn) eke out a pathetic existence on the Upper West Side of Manhattan. Bobby is a small-time drug dealer and occasional user; Helen wants to get a real job but quits as a waitress in a Broadway coffee shop when she can't put up with the demanding customers. When the two are locked out of their residential hotel room for nonpayment of rent, they sleep wherever they can. Helen eventually succumbs to trying heroin to temporarily

Bobby and Helen talk about past and future in the park.

Bobby helps pack up some heroin in Harlem.

Pacino and Winn take a break during the shooting of *The Panic in Needle Park.*

escape her bleak existence and becomes hooked on it. From then on things get worse and worse for the couple: She turns to prostitution to support her habit; he gets arrested while helping his brother during a robbery. Months later, Helen "rats" on Bobby to a sympathetic narc (Alan Vint) in order to avoid imprisonment. Bobby is put back in the joint ("Cunt! I was gonna marry you!" he screams at her, as if he were some prize), but Helen is waiting for him when he is released. They walk off together, companions in nightmare till death do them part.

All of this is played out with often unnerving realism, particularly scenes showing assorted junkies shooting themselves up (both in long shot and close-up; no cutaways saying, "It's only actors") and immediately zonking out into whatever dreamland awaits them; or a long sequence in which Pacino watches as the heroin is cut, carefully measured, and rapidly packaged behind the deceptively prosaic wooden doors of a Harlem apartment.

Although the picture employs a shapeless, formless cinéma vérité approach (which doesn't always work), the filmmakers were hardly hippie documentarians. Director Jerry Schatzberg had previously directed the glossy study of a fashion model, *Puzzle of a Downfall Child*, the year before. (A former fashion photographer, Schatzberg starred his then girlfriend Faye Dunaway in that film). Producer Dominick Dunne now writes glitzy tales of the rich and powerful in *Vanity Fair* and in such novels as *The Two Mrs. Grenvilles*. These were odd choices to put together a film about such drab, outré, disreputable New York denizens; it is to their credit that they avoided any and all sentimentalization or glamorization of the downbeat, lurid subject matter.

Although the picture begins slowly, it soon rivets with some excellent sequences and telling details. When Helen gets a letter from her mother, Bobby's first response is to open the envelope to see inside. "Any bread?" he asks hopefully. Playing stickball with Helen and some neighborhood youngsters, Bobby grabs her in an exuberant hug and then notices that look in her eyes that indicates she's crossed over the fatal line into addiction. "When did that happen?" he asks.

A particularly lively and funny-ugly scene has Pacino passing out at a woman's apartment. The woman, who, like Helen, turns tricks to support her habit, is expecting a john any minute and is panicking that

he'll be frightened away by the other people, not to mention Pacino's body. "He can't die here!" she screams as her baby wails in the background and Helen and a pal try desperately to revive Bobby. An even more grotesque scene has Bobby and Helen shooting up in the men's room of the Staten Island Ferry as the little dog they just got runs off by itself to examine the boat. They come out of the men's room just in time to witness the dog jumping off the back of the ferry and drowning. (The trouble is that the sequence borders on black comedy, and Helen's reaction, her hitting Bobby and crying hysterically, should have been strengthened and expanded.)

Pacino's performance in his first starring role is excellent, exhibiting the ability and charisma that would carry him to even greater heights in years to come. Clearly, he put much of himself, his early struggle to survive, into the role of Bobby (although Bobby, unlike Pacino, is essentially a loser). Pacino looks oddly "geeky" in the opening scenes but is still attractive and masculine, "lethal" to the ladies; one can see why his Bobby exudes a fatal attraction over poor Helen, whose attachment to him is her downfall.

The Pacino charm is also in evidence, such as when he sneaks into the hospital against nurses' orders to see Helen and makes her smile; or when he gets extra money from an old lady pawnbroker. "I'm dying of dope," he tells her. "I'm dying of hunger," she replies.

Although Pacino is a bit too intelligent and "cultured" a person to be 100 percent convincing as a hopeless lowlife, he does register at an admirable 98 percent, and his performance betrays no *controllable* false notes at all.

The Panic in Needle Park is the first film in which Pacino unleashes his patented Pacino blast, the one moment when he really hauls off, busts ass, and *explodes*. This occurs when he learns that Helen has been selling her body to support her eighty-dollar-a-day drug habit. Running from his blows, Helen bolts into the bathroom and locks the door. Hollering and cursing, Pacino pounds the door and threatens to break it down. This was only the first of many Pacino blasts in subsequent pictures.

Kitty Winn is also admirable as poor Helen. She had won raves playing *Saint Joan* in San Francisco at the American Conservatory Theater, and her performance in *The Panic in Needle Park* garnered her a Best Actress prize at the 1971 Cannes Film Festival. It's a shame that we never learn more of her character's motives for leaving home. "I was born and went to school," she says of her former life. "I had a mother and a father and a little brother and a lawn. I was always going to art classes, and my mother was always going to the doctor. It was all right."

All right, maybe, but not enough. Helen is one of those girls who leaves home to seek adventure, excitement, something different, but hasn't the determination or drive or wherewithal to have a goal or any kind of realistic game plan. Too many wind up lost or dead or buried in unmarked graves or, like Helen, in thrall to a man who is no good because of weaknesses of their own.

Richard Bright also scores as Bobby's burglarizing brother, Hank, who looks so respectable in suit and tie when we first see him but who reveals his true

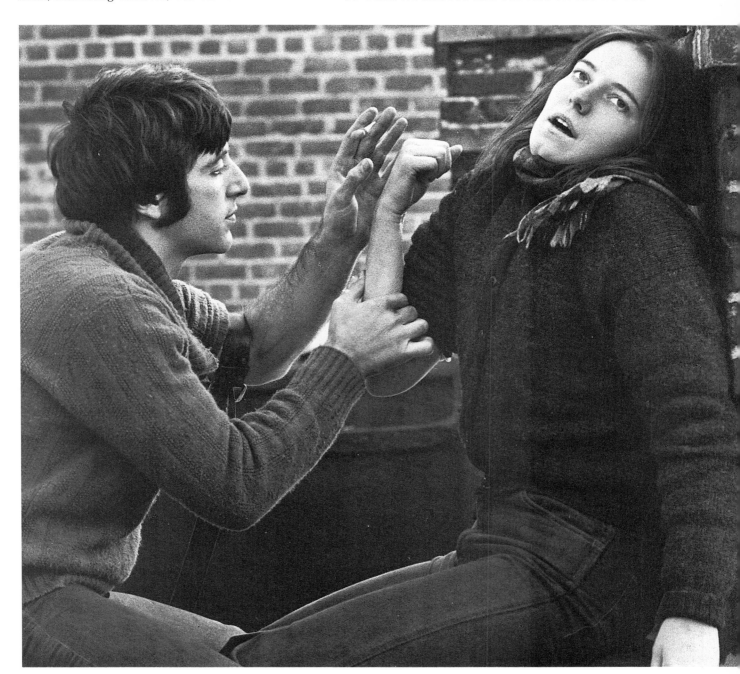

Getting high on heroin: the beginning of the end.

A strung-out Helen shows the effects of drug abuse, but Bobby barely notices.

nature when we hear his low-class accent (more common than Pacino's) and see the missing teeth when he smiles. Hank is just as much on the outside as his brother is.

Smaller roles are played by Raul Julia as an artist-friend of Bobby's and Paul Sorvino as a john who is robbed of twenty-five dollars by Helen. Alan Vint is fine as a police officer, Hotch, who tries to pry Helen away from Bobby for her own sake and his; Dora Weissman and Bryant Fraser also make their mark in the film as, respectively, the likable old lady in the pawnshop and a young preppie who buys Helen's body but winds up giving a threatening Bobby all of his money.

Adam Holender's photography—atmospheric shots of Seventy-second Street and Broadway and its environs, lots of close-ups of needles and other drug paraphernalia—is appropriately murky. Never has Manhattan looked so drab and ugly. There is no musical score—music would have helped create some pathos—but lots of background noise, which adds to the veracity of the picture but occasionally almost drowns out the dialogue.

The Panic in Needle Park is an absorbing but ultimately minor work. Great stories can be told about

Screwed-up Bobby and Helen get a dog while visiting Staten Island. The poor pooch never makes it to Manhattan.

48

strugglers and losers in New York City, but this lacks sympathetic characters who have a purpose and (thwarted) goals. Bobby and Helen are primarily responsible for their own problems; there is nothing remotely "heroic" about either of them, which is perhaps the point.

The Panic in Needle Park also lacks that certain *depth* which distinguishes other (often foreign) studies of losers, misfits, and lowlifes, such as Britain's *Leather Boys*.

Still, the film was to lead to bigger and better projects for Pacino.

THE GODFATHER

Paramount, 1972

Producer, Albert S. Ruddy; director, Francis Ford Coppola; director of photography, Gordon Willis; editors, William Reynolds, and Peter Zinner; screenplay, Coppola and Mario Puzo; based on the novel by Mario Puzo; associate producer, Gray Frederickson; music, Nino Rota; production designer, Dean Tavoularis; costume designer, Anna Hill Johnstone; hairstylist, Phil Leto. Running time: 171 min.

CAST

Marlon Brando (*Don Corleone*); Al Pacino (*Michael Corleone*); Diane Keaton (*Kay Adams*); Robert Duvall (*Tom Hagen*); James Caan (*Sonny Corleone*); John Cazale (*Fredo Corleone*); Talia Shire (*Connie*); Gianni Russo (*Carlo*); Lenny Montana (*Luca Brasi*); John Marley (*Paulie Gatlo*); Alex Rocco (*Moe Green*); Richard Conte (*Barzini*); Simonetta Stefanelli (*Appollonia*); Abe Vigoda (*Tessio*); Sterling Hayden (*Captain McCluskey*); Al Martino (*Johnny Fontaine*); Al Lettieri (*Solfozzo*); Tony Giorgio (*Bruno Tattaglia*); Richard Castellano (*Clemenza*).

After a lot of hassle—somebody made Pacino "an offer he couldn't refuse" (the picture made that phrase part of our national language)—Pacino took the part of Michael Corleone in the film version of Mario Puzo's best-seller, and the rest is history. This was the film that catapulted Pacino into stardom.

In post–World War II New York, Don Vito Corleone (Marlon Brando) is the godfather of the Italian mob. His two sons Sonny (James Caan) and Fredo (John Cazale) are part and parcel of the family business. His adopted son, Tom Hagan (Robert Duvall), acts as the family lawyer but is generally kept outside of the dirtier parts of the business. Corleone's third son, Michael, who enlisted in the service, has an independent mind and at first wants nothing to do with the family trade.

The Corleones are, if possible, "good"—and self-justifying—mobsters. They only traffic in the "harmless" vices of gambling and prostitution. When someone points out that "senators and presidents don't have men killed," they accuse the speaker of naïveté. Don Corleone doesn't want to get into the "dirty business" of drug dealing not because of the innocents who will be corrupted but because his "friends in high places" won't be able to look the other way, as they do with his less controversial (if equally illegal) activities.

Don Corleone's not-so-noble-minded refusal to traffic in narcotics leads to a war between crime families, with the don himself nearly the first casualty. Seeing his family under attack, Michael develops a new attitude: He himself will assassinate two of their enemies, who will be taken completely by surprise. This sets him down a completely different road from the one he had intended to travel, and before long his corrup-

The Godfather introduced Al Pacino to the widest possible audience.

51

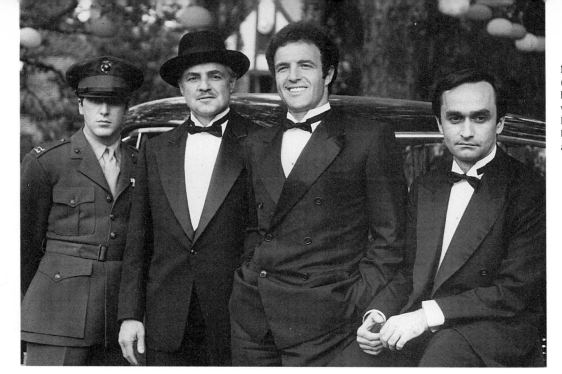

Michael Corleone (Pacino, *far left*) is home from the war with his father (Marlon Brando) and two brothers (James Caan and John Cazale).

tion is complete. He takes over the family and is soon eliminating all enemies just as ruthlessly as his father before him. The new godfather, it seems, has grown quite comfortable in his role.

Completely absorbing during its nearly three-hour running time, *The Godfather* has plenty of colorfully gruesome and flavorful highlights to punctuate the many scenes of mafioso talking and planning and vowing vengeance and havoc. One of the first murders is of Corleone henchman Luca (Lenny Montana), who has a quiet drink with members of the drug cartel in a deserted bar. Suddenly, one of the men plunges a knife through his hand and into the bar counter below it, pinning his hand to the bar, while another strangles him from behind. A more quiet murder has another Corleone henchman, Paulie (John Martino), shot in the back of the head by an associate (in the distant background) as family friend Clemenza (Richard Castellano), who ordered the hit, urinates into some bushes at the side of the road in the foreground. Not only do these mobsters talk about murder casually, they even *enact* it that way.

Sonny's murder at the tollbooth on the causeway is also exciting, as are the events leading up to it. First, Sonny's sister Connie (Talia Shire) has a plate-smashing free-for-all with her slick, no-good husband, Carlo (Gianni Russo), who has sold out to the Corleones' enemies. Carlo takes a belt to Connie, knowing that when news of his actions reach Sonny's ears, he'll jump into his car and head straight for him to avenge

The extravagant Italian wedding that begins *The Godfather*.

his sister. However, the rival faction has set up an ambush at the tollbooth, and Sonny is riddled with so many bullets that it's a miracle (and a bit implausible) that he manages to last as long as he does. Before he expires, defiant to the last, Sonny manages to get a few licks in himself.

The most suspenseful passage in the film details the double assassination that sends Michael spiraling downward into a life of corruption and brutality. Michael insists that he be allowed to meet with the head of the drug faction and a sinister police captain who has been bought by the Mob. The site of the meeting is a down-market Italian restaurant where a gun has been hidden in one of the stalls in the men's room. Michael excuses himself from the table, gets the gun, and after a few moments of trepidation, steps out to blast away at both completely surprised adversaries.

Pacino's acting certainly helps maintain the high

While his daughter and new son-in-law celebrate, Don Corleone (Marlon Brando) takes requests from relatives in trouble.

degree of tension in this scene. When first we see him, during his sister's wedding at the opening of the film, he displays a kind of scrubbed innocence, a healthy attention to grooming, and a basic decency that is in sharp contrast to his "Bobby" character in *The Panic in Needle Park*. As the picture progresses, however, he slowly becomes more authoritative and menacing. Driving to the restaurant with the police captain and his druggie chum, his face betrays a growing amorality, hardened determination, and seeping viciousness that has wiped out all traces of innocence. Pacino looks convincingly tense and nervous before committing the double hit—but not guilt-wracked. Michael Corleone has crossed over, and there's no turning back.

Although Marlon Brando probably got more press (and certainly more money), Pacino is clearly the film's true star and has the pivotal role; it's a charismatic, star-making performance. Oddly enough considering the subject matter, there is no Pacino blast in the film. Instead of screeching and kicking the furniture (that Pacino leaves to James Caan's Sonny), Pacino underplays through most of the picture; whether making a casino owner an offer he can't refuse (he wants to buy him out and *that's that*) or questioning his terrified quisling brother-in-law Carlo, Pacino is the essence of menacing cool.

Interspersed with the bloody action, the picture has a lot of *talk*. In these quieter moments Pacino shows what a good listener he can be, such as when he talks patiently to an increasingly confused Don Corleone in the garden. (Brando himself is charming as he clowns with his grandson in the garden moments before suffering a fatal heart attack.)

Speaking of Brando, *The Godfather* was his big comeback film, and he shocked everyone by con-

A tense scene as Michael prepares to murder Captain McCluskey (Sterling Hayden) and drug kingpin Sollozzo (Al Lettieri).

Johnny Fontaine (Al Martino)— said to be inspired by Frank Sinatra —takes another kind of request as Connie Corleone (Talia Shire) sits and listens.

senting to audition for the role. Opinion was sharply divided as to the veracity of his performance. He does play Don Corleone with appropriate toughness and virility—he retains his great presence—but that voice! His cheeks stuffed with jowl-creating cotton or the like, Brando sometimes sounds like Daffy Duck and is often nearly unintelligible. (That didn't stop him from winning an Academy Award as Best Actor!)

Pacino had to settle for a nomination as Best Supporting Actor (as did Duvall and Caan)—a dubious honor at best. Pacino was far more than "support" for Brando. His, in fact, was the lead role, the "Godfather" of the title. For the record, Coppola was nominated for his direction but won for his screenplay (cowritten with Mario Puzo). *The Godfather* earned an Oscar for Best Picture.

But the sum of *The Godfather*'s parts don't really add up to a whole. Audiences and critics were so entertained by the fast-paced, larger-than-life story and film that it escaped many that *The Godfather* is an "amusing" potboiler but hardly a work of art. Francis Ford Coppola is no William Wyler; there isn't the care in each shot and setup that would indicate truly *great* filmmaking. *The Godfather* plays like a parody at times—the severed horse's head found in the uncooperative director's bed, for instance—but it lacks a subtext of *humanity*, people that we could root for and care about.

55

Michael has a quiet chat in the garden with his father.

56

After the double murders, Michael has to hide out in Sicily. Here he talks with a bodyguard.

Meanwhile, back in the States, brother Sonny (James Caan) gives wife-beating brother-in-law Carlo (Gianni Russo) a piece of his fists.

The Godfather is packed with talented supporting players such as Richard Conte as mafioso Barzini.

Still, a great many talented people made significant contributions to *The Godfather*'s success. In addition to the aforementioned fine actors, Diane Keaton, as Michael's wife, is expressive and generally believable. Although his Tom Hagen isn't personally involved in any killings, Robert Duvall hints at the sociopathology hiding just behind the surface. Al Lettieri really scores as the sleazy drug kingpin Sollozzo, and Richard Castellano hits the mark as the "lovable" Clemenza, who talks about killing people as he stirs his spaghetti sauce. All the supporting roles—from John Cazale's "Fredo" and Talia Shire's "Connie" down to Al Martino's Johnny Fontaine (said to be inspired by Frank Sinatra) and Sterling Hayden's Captain McCluskey—have been cast with great care and felicitous results.

Production designer Dean Tavoularis and costume designer Anna Hill Johnstone conspired to re-create a believable New York—and Nevada (where the family relocates)—of the 1940s. But hairstylist Phil Leto should have been run out of town; most of the "boys" sport haircuts that would have been more appropriate to the 1950s or 1960s than the postwar period! They are much too long and shaggy. Why did director Coppola let Leto get away with such an anachronism?

Gordon Willis's photography is mostly first-rate; there are particularly beautiful shots of Sicily and the town of Corleone, where Michael goes to hide after the double assassination. Nino Rota has written a good, effective score for the picture; it has a sinister quality that adds to the tension and functions as a "storm warning." His famous theme music for the film is also quite memorable. However, some of the best music comes from other sources. The "Brindisi" (or drinking song) from Verdi's *La Traviata* plays during the second wedding sequence, and the music of J. S. Bach does the same during the film's climactic baptism.

The Godfather elicited some criticism as to the possibility that it romanticized the Mafia. To a certain extent this is true—the movie is a somewhat cosmeticized study of lowlifes, making these sordid people seem like characters in an opera (not that every character in an opera is *nice*)—but essentially the film resists making true heroes out of these scumbags. Case in point? The aforementioned baptism of Michael's

Michael Corleone is the new don, but these gangsters treat him like the pope.

nephew in a bucolic church, which is splendidly intercut with scenes of hit men putting paid to various enemies of the Corleone family in several well-orchestrated strokes. As we see murder after murder occurring in quick spurts, the camera always returns us to that church, where the new godfather swears to forgo all sin and evil even as dozens of assassinations he ordered are being carried out. (Only a short while later Michael even orders the murder of the baptized child's *father!*) This important sequence, the best in the movie, seems to say: these people, *heroes*? Forget it!

But for Al Pacino, it was only the beginning.

Pacino as a dapper young don.

Michael and Sonny have supper with some associates.

SCARECROW

Warner Brothers, 1973

Producer, Robert M. Sherman; director, Jerry Schatzberg; director of photography, Vilmos Zsigmond; editor, Evan Lottman; screenplay, Garry Michael White; music, Fred Myrow; assistant director, Tom Shaw; production designer, Al Brenner; costume designer, Jo Ynocencio. Running time: 115 min.

Pacino stars as Francis—a.k.a. Lion—in *Scarecrow*.

CAST

Al Pacino (*Lion*); Gene Hackman (*Max*); Dorothy Tristan (*Coley*); Ann Wedgeworth (*Frenchy*); Richard Lynch (*Riley*); Penny Allen (*Annie*); Eileen Brennan (*Darlene*); Richard Hackman (*Mickey*); Al Cingoiani (*Skipper*); Rutanya Aida (*Woman in Camper*).

Pacino was back working with director Jerry (*The Panic in Needle Park*) Schatzberg in *Scarecrow,* in which he was teamed with a post–*French Connection* Gene Hackman for this *Midnight Cowboy*–influenced American Odyssey.

Max (Hackman) has just come out of San Quentin and is heading for Pittsburgh, where he plans to open a car wash. Another hitchhiker, Francis (Al Pacino), whom he meets on the road, is heading to Detroit after a stint in the navy. Francis, whom Max insists on calling "Lion" (short for his middle name, Lionel), is

Gene Hackman is Max in *Scarecrow*.

Lion and Max become good buddies while sharing a meal at a greasy spoon.

naively hoping for a happy reunion with the woman he ran out on as well as his first glance of their child, whose sex he does not know.

After a stopover in Denver to spend time with Max's cousin—and a few weeks of incarceration due to a bar fight—the buddies arrive in Detroit, where Francis's ex-girlfriend, Annie (Penny Allen), tells him that their son died before he could be born or baptized. (She's lying; the six-year-old boy is actually playing beside her.) Suffering a delayed reaction to this devastating news, Francis has a nervous breakdown while playing with some small children at a public fountain.

Francis is institutionalized. Max buys a round-trip ticket to Pittsburgh. He has come to care deeply for "Lion" and will use the money with which he planned to finance his car wash to make sure Francis gets proper treatment.

While not quite *Of Mice and Men*—or its obvious model, *Midnight Cowboy*—*Scarecrow* is a rather affecting study of mediocrity in the human species. Its characters are almost exclusively drifters, losers, and jailbirds, but somehow the picture touches a chord and at times achieves a certain poignancy. This is due in large part to Pacino's touching performance as the hapless Francis.

Pacino's "Lion" is a lovable schnook and borderline simpleton. His philosophy toward life (and the meaning of the title) is: "You don't have to fight people if you make 'em laugh." In his view crows aren't scared of scarecrows. "They make 'em laugh. They think the farmer's a good guy and fly on by." Max admits that he finally warmed up to him on the highway (Francis tried all sorts of tricks to ingratiate himself with the taciturn Max) not only because Lion gave him his last match but because "you made me laugh."

This opening highway scene shows Pacino at his

most charming. Standing across the road from Max, Francis is determined to make the fellow respond to him. He jumps up and down like a monkey, digs in his ear with a thumb and pretends his hand is a telephone, screams obscenities at the cars that pass them by. Francis is a sweet person who only wants to be liked. Although he behaved irresponsibly with his pregnant girlfriend (one can't see Francis being very successful at the husband-and-daddy bit), he was thoughtful enough to send money home on a regular basis. But while Francis may think he's ready for an instant family, Annie—who was married in the interim—is too bitter to play along.

Pacino is terrific in *Scarecrow*; he almost makes it all seem effortless. His Francis is irresistible; his need to be liked and his irrepressible good humor in the face of adversity, admirable. In the prison-camp sequences, Max seems to blame Lion for their incarceration, although it was quick-with-his-fists Maxie who started the fight. Driving past a pigpen with a smitten trustee (who wants Francis to help him put on a prison show), Lion sees Max feeding slop to the pigs and quips, "Us show people sure do envy yo' simple folk of de land," giving the line an almost campy insouciance.

Speaking of the trustee, Riley (Richard Lynch), Lion's later encounter with him shows that he can't always count on his sense of humor to get him out of tight places. While sharing a quiet drink with Francis, Riley tries to kiss him and, when rebuffed, gets angry. Doing a right-on-the-nose imitation of Boris Karloff ("Go back, Igor! Go back!"), Lion tries to make light of the whole incident, sparing Riley's feelings, but Riley is too determined to get what he wants. When Lion refuses to go down on him, Riley beats him within an inch of his life. Throughout this long sequence Pacino plays with absolute conviction: a nice guy faced with an impossible situation, not wanting to hurt or offend but completely unable to comply with an unfair demand and suffering because of it.

Although he avoids being raped, this is the first time Lion is unable to get out of a scrap with his sense of humor, and it sobers him. Later on, Maxie uses this method to avoid a fight with a bar punk—he does an impromptu striptease that has the joint in an uproar and leaves the punk nonplussed—but Francis's face, watching, betrays only world-weariness and a fatigue of the spirit that hints at the breakdown to come. This occurs when he's doing a spirited pirate imitation for some kids at a water fountain. Suddenly, he walks

into the fountain carrying a young boy—to the child's delight and his mother's consternation—and completely loses it. (Pacino seems a little self-conscious in this scene but is effective.)

Scarecrow is saved from complete depression by several infusions of comedy relief. One has Maxie hollering at barfly Darlene (Eileen Brennan) as she sits in a seedy dive but winding up dragging her home while Lion follows with a department-store dummy in tow. Trying to get work in a restaurant, the two buddies are bodily thrown out of the kitchen by chattering,

Max and Lion wonder what's next on the horizon.

Max and Lion hitch a ride in back of a truck.

furious Hispanics. The funniest sequence has Hackman requesting Pacino to provide a distraction so he can shoplift a couple of purses in a department store. Lion's distraction—he runs all over the store like a maniac or a gridiron hero on uppers—is *so* distracting that Maxie forgets to hide the purses under his jacket. After the breakup of one of several bar fights in the picture, Lion and Maxie wind up dancing together. (But no, the picture seems devoid of genuinely homo-erotic overtones.)

Gene Hackman's performance is almost as good as Pacino's. To his credit, he never overplays or lapses into sentimentalizing his character. Some critics complained that Hackman remained too cold and aloof, too distant from Pacino, but Hackman was probably aware that his paranoid, prickly Maxie was not exactly a likable person or one who warmed up to people very easily. The picture's final sequence, with Maxie buying a round-trip instead of one-way ticket, is supposed to show how he has *changed*.

Max and Lion arrive in yet another town on their sojourn.

Al Pacino, as Lion, entertains inmates during a
prison show.

Lion and Max "beat feet"
on their way to destiny.

Eileen Brennan is as much fun as ever, and Richard Lynch—one of our most reliable character actors—makes the most of the horny trustee bent on having his way with Pacino. Ann Wedgeworth, as Frenchy, who has a yen herself for Hackman's (rather hidden) charms, does the same sexy, vague "bimbo" routine that she's done from this picture up until the TV show *Evening Shade* nearly twenty years later. Wedgeworth is good—but talk about typecast!

After Pacino and Hackman, the acting honors have to go to Penny Allen, who has the small bit as Lion's girlfriend, Annie. When Lion calls her on the phone after a several-year absence and she recognizes his voice, she puts more into the word "Francis?" than lesser actresses have done with entire monologues. Her superb reaction is sustained throughout the conversation, in which she reveals that she got married to a man known in town as the Banana King. "Am I happy?" she says to Francis with exquisite bitterness. "I'm Mrs. Joey Banana King, and I look like an old lady!" Allen makes her character instantly sympathetic, but we can also see why Francis left her.

The extras and bit players in *Scarecrow*—those haunted midnight denizens of bars soaking up alcohol to ease their disappointment—capture the drunken good times of losers very vividly. (If movie extras don't know about disappointment, who does?)

Max does an impromptu striptease in a bar as Lion—way in the background, near the exit—watches.

Friends forever: Max and Lion. (Hackman and Pacino were not friends, however.)

Fred Myrow has written some nice jazz rifts for the picture—his horns and drums matching the beat of the window wipers in the police car as our heroes are taken to jail is an inspired touch—but it is Vilmos Zsigmond's superb cinematography that really helps put *Scarecrow* over. From picture-postcard country lanes to rat-infested auto junkyards, from sunny, flat highways to smoky, crowded gin joints, Zsigmond provides atmospheric vistas of an America both pretty and *grim*.

Garry Michael White's screenplay was attacked for its obvious symbolism and pretentious aspects—and the risqué humor seems more the stuff of sitcoms with each passing year—but it is a more than workable script. With its screwed-up people, wasted lives, and embittered characters hurting each other in both casual and deliberate manners, *Scarecrow* works up some evocative pathos and hints at things perhaps better left unspoken.

Pacino won the Best Actor prize at Cannes for his work in *Scarecrow*, which he fully deserved.

SERPICO

Paramount; a Dino De Laurentiis presentation,
1973

Producer, Martin Bregman; director, Sidney Lumet;
director of photography, Arthur J. Ornitz; editor, Dede
Allen; screenplay, Waldo Salt and Norman Wexler;
based on the book by Peter Maas; associate producer,
Roger M. Rothstein; music, Mikis Theodorakis. Running time: 130 min.

CAST

Al Pacino (*Frank Serpico*); John Randolph (*Sidney
Green*); Cornelia Sharpe (*Leslie*); Biff McGuire (*Captain McClain*); Barbara Eda Young (*Laurie*); Jack
Kehoe (*Tom Keough*); Tony Roberts (*Bob Blair*); Norman Ornellas (*Rubello*); Ed Grover (*Inspector Lombardo*); Richard Foronjy (*Corsaro*); Mildred Clinton
(*Mrs. Serpico*).

Frank Serpico was like a synthesis of Pacino's Lionel
in *Scarecrow* and Michael Corleone in *The Godfather*.
Like the former, he was an essentially decent, if imper-
fect, human being. Like the latter, he has definite goals
and a certain amount of "seedy" polish. Otherwise,
he is nothing like Michael Corleone.

Frank Serpico was a real-life cop who blew the
whistle on corruption in the police department and

Al Pacino as Frank Serpico; Pacino received an Academy Award
nomination for his performance and won the Golden Globe
Award as Best Actor.

nearly paid for it with his life. He is a man of principle
and initiative. Pacino was attracted to his story and
wanted to play the part, particularly after meeting the
man himself, who impressed him mightily.

Frank Serpico is a fresh-faced kid straight out of
the police academy with a naive attitude toward law
enforcement. Gradually, he develops a grungy sophis-
tication and becomes a maverick on the force. He
wears his hair too long and grows a mustache. He
listens to opera and demonstrates ballet steps in the
precinct. He carries a small white mouse around with
him wherever he goes. When some of his more "ma-

Serpico graduates from the policy academy with fellow officers.

cho" colleagues in the B.C.I. (Bureau of Criminal Investigation) assume he's gay, he winds up transferred to the plainclothes division, where his hair and mustache will be more appropriate.

One day he is handed an envelope with money in it, but Serpico wants no part of payoffs. "Who can trust a cop who don't take money?" someone tells him. Frank is appalled to learn that one precinct alone is collecting $250,000 a year in payola. He is a rare bird, a cop who thinks the police should spend their energy fighting crime and not collecting payoffs. Informed of the situation, the mayor is afraid to alienate the police force because he anticipates a summer of riots. Serpico takes out his frustration on his girlfriend.

A special commission is set up to investigate the problem, but Serpico is afraid it will go after the small fries but ignore the big guns, like the commissioner, "who knew about it for years and did *nothing*." Serpico tells his story to the *New York Times* and is promptly switched to narcotics, where he is set up during a drug bust and shot. He survives but loses hearing in one ear. Offered a gold shield, he turns it down and resigns from the force, moving to Switzerland.

Serpico was eventually awarded a "medal of honor for conspicuous bravery in action."

Serpico takes a while to pick up under Sydney Lumet's styleless direction but eventually becomes grittily absorbing. Pacino, at the height of his appeal and attractiveness, looks suitably fresh-scrubbed and innocent as a young cadet and convincingly grungy and disgusted as the story proceeds; it is a notable performance.

The picture gives Pacino plenty of opportunities to display the Pacino blast. Threatening to implode under all the pressure and going crazy from frustration, he hollers at his girlfriend: "Clean this place up! I don't want to pick up shit!" When Captain McClain (Biff McGuire) goes ballistic when he learns that Serpico is going to an outside agency with what he knows—"We wash our own laundry!" McClain screams—Pacino blasts back: *"We don't!"*

By far the most impressive blast—and the best scene in the picture—occurs when Serpico arrests Corsaro (Rochard Foronjy) and brings him back to the precinct for processing. As Serpico runs around with the paperwork, Corsaro sits and jokes with the other cops

Frank Serpico and his mother (Mildred Clinton) on graduation day.

Serpico is too unconventional to please his fellow cops.

Serpico levels with a suspect.

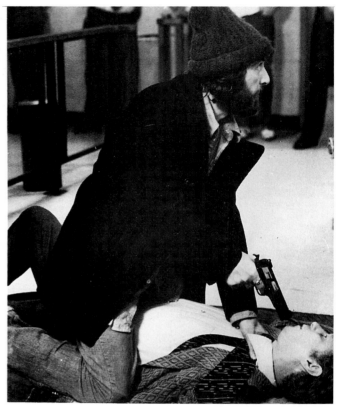

Serpico rides his bike with girlfriend Leslie (Cornelia Sharpe).

Serpico is in no mood to be messed with.

Serpico rushes into action with a fellow officer.

Serpico's buddy Bob Blair (Tony Roberts) agrees to help him expose police corruption.

behind his back. (The acting of Richard Foronjy, quite cocky and vivid in mustache and panama hat, adds immeasurably to the success of the sequence.) When Serpico sees what is happening, he is infuriated. "This man did fifteen years for killing a cop," he hollers (or words to that effect) "and you assholes are palling around with him!" First he picks up Corsaro and slams him into the holding cage. Then he steps back into the room and literally starts throwing chairs around, a frightening spectacle in his completely justified outrage.

No one can hold a candle to Pacino when he is

throwing the furniture (and maybe chewing the scenery, some might suggest).

Pacino is surrounded by other fine actors in *Serpico*. Ed Grover gives a good account of himself as Inspector Lombardo, a tough, tired, but honest cop and the only guy at the Sixth Precinct who will work with Serpico. John Randolph is excellent, as usual, as the head of the task force gathered to investigate Serpico's claims. Jack Kehoe, Norman Ornellas, and Biff McGuire all register as some of Serpico's associates. Tony Roberts seems a bit out of place as a friend who tries to help Serpico get justice. Barbara Eda Young is a bit too

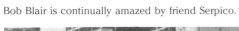
Bob Blair is continually amazed by friend Serpico.

Serpico looks out over the city that he loves.

Serpico and associate are getting ready for action.

Serpico better watch out: Everyone is out to get him.

low-key as Serpico's second girlfriend, failing to make the most of their confrontation, although Cornelia Sharpe is fine as the first girlfriend, Leslie. Mildred Clinton, who briefly plays Serpico's mother with warmth and humanity, was to really click four years later as the deranged "Mrs. Tredoni" in Alfred Sole's shocker *Communion*.

Despite the intense tone and grim subject matter, *Serpico* does have its lighter moments, such as when Serpico sings (?) an aria from Puccini's *Gianni Schicchi* as he drives to work. (Placido Domingo has nothing to fear from Al Pacino.) And a scene when Serpico and other cops are told to light up some joints so they can "learn" about grass is hilarious because it is obvious that most of them have already been stoned on marijuana many times!

Arthur J. Ornitz's photography of various New York City locations, from Gay Street in Greenwich Village (where Serpico lives) to the meat-market district at Ninth Avenue, are more than adequate, but Mikis Theodorakis's brassy score does absolutely nothing for the picture.

Pacino received an Academy Award nomination as Best Actor; he copped the Golden Globe Award, however. This time there was no Brando or Hackman to share the spotlight with. Pacino was a star—the sole star—in his own right.

THE GODFATHER, PART II

Paramount, 1974

Al Pacino as Michael Corleone in *The Godfather, Part II.*

Producer, Francis Ford Coppola; director, Coppola; director of photography, Gordon Willis; editors, Peter Zinner, A.C.E., Barry Malkin, and Richard Marks; screenplay, Coppola and Mario Puzo; based on *The Godfather* by Puzo; music, Nino Rota; coproducers, Gray Frederickson and Fred Roos; associate producer, Mona Skager; production designer, Dean Tavoularis; costume designer, Theodora Van Runkle. Running time: 200 min.

CAST

Al Pacino (*Michael Corleone*); Robert De Niro (*Vito Corleone*); Diane Keaton (*Kay*); John Cazale (*Fredo*); Robert Duvall (*Tom Hagen*); Talia Shire (*Connie*); G. D. Spradlin (*Pat Geary*); Mariana Hill (*Deanna*); Michael V. Gazzo (*Frankie*); Lee Strasberg (*Hyman Roth*); Dominic Chianese (*Johnny Ola*); B. Kirby Jr. (*Young Clemenza*); Gaston Moschin (*Don Fanucci*); Troy Donahue (*Merle Johnson*); Joe Spinell (*Cicci*); Leopoldo Trieste (*Don Roberto*); Roger Corman (*Senator Number 2*).

How to continue the saga of the Corleone family? wondered producer-director-cowriter Francis Ford Coppola. The future? The past? Why not both?

It was decided that *The Godfather, Part II* would be a two-part film: One would be a "prequel" showing how the original godfather, Vito Corleone (played in the original film by Marlon Brando), came to power; the second would be a sequel continuing the adventures of new godfather Michael Corleone (Al Pacino).

For the plum role of Vito Corleone as a young man, a relative unknown named Robert De Niro was chosen. There was no thought of replacing Al Pacino with anyone else in the role of Vito's son Michael.

Left, Michael Corleone runs the family business now. *Right,* Kay Corleone (Diane Keaton) reminds Michael that he hasn't kept his promise to get out of the business within five years.

Rather than show an hour and a half of the prequel and then an hour and a half of the sequel, the two story lines were intercut, moving back and forth through time at significant moments in the lives of the characters. It was an effective way of linking father and son, showing how each dealt with problems and did away with adversaries in similarly ruthless fashion.

In the prequel, Vito Andolini is born in the Sicilian town of Corleone in 1901. By his ninth birthday, Vito's brother, father, and mother have all been murdered by the local don. Vito escapes to America, where an immigration official mistakes the name of the town he comes from for his surname. Years later, Vito is married and living in Little Italy in New York, a neighborhood controlled by Don Fanucci (Gaston Moschin) of the Black Hand. Fanucci has a stranglehold on the local merchants with his protection racket. When Fanucci insists that the owner of the store where Vito works replace Vito with his nephew, Vito turns to house robbing with a friend. When the don asks for a cut, Vito murders him and takes over his activities. He returns briefly to Sicily to kill the godfather who wiped out the rest of his family.

The sequel takes place mostly in Lake Tahoe in 1958, where Michael masquerades as a successful hotel owner. His promise to his wife, Kay (Diane Keaton), to get out of the family business within five years has not been kept. Attacked in his own bedroom by gunmen, who nearly hit his wife and child, Michael vows to destroy those both inside and outside his operation who put his family in danger. More ruthless than his father ever was, Michael wipes out rival factions and even orders a hit on his own brother, Fredo (John Cazale), who has "innocently" given potent information to their enemies. A disgusted Kay walks out on Michael, leaving him a godfather alone except for adopted brother Tom Hagen (Robert Duvall) and his sister, Connie (Talia Shire), who has forgiven him for murdering her husband.

Some sections of *The Godfather, Part II* have an undeniable sheen of class and artistry, an unmistakably polished craftmanship, that is all the more ironic, since it is several cuts below the original. Considering that two years had gone by since they saw the first film, most audiences didn't notice. Besides, they were riveted by several top-notch sequences, most dealing with the gruesome dispatching of several individuals no one would miss.

For instance, there's Vito Corleone's murder of Don Fanucci, with the former waiting beside the stairs as the latter slowly and confidently ascends to his apartment. Fanucci thinks himself master of all he surveys and has no inkling that the arrogant Vito is waiting in the shadows. With a towel over his hand to hide the gun, Vito walks into the don's apartment, shoots him, then calmly goes home to his wife and babies as if nothing had ever happened. While Fanucci is hardly an innocent victim, it is also clear that there is something of the sociopath in Vito Corleone's makeup.

Another "fun" scene has loudmouth Frankie (Michael V. Gazzo), a renegade member of the family, being garroted in the back of a bar just as a policeman decides to step into the place for a drink. The timely intervention of the flatfoot saves Frankie's life (for the moment) but leads to an exciting shootout on the street.

One victim who doesn't deserve what she gets is Vito's mother, who early in the picture confronts the Sicilian don who has murdered one son and husband for an alleged insult to his family. She begs him to spare her youngest child, Vito, but the don is unmoved. He knows young Vito will want to kill him as soon as he is able. Right in front of the boy the mother's throat is slashed, an act which, we assume, must have a psychological impact on the lad. (The *Godfather* movies are potboilers which rarely, if ever, delve into the psychological motivations of the characters.)

As in the first picture, perhaps the best sequence in the sequel is the climactic montage in which all of the godfather's prime enemies are taken care of in a

Michael confers with gangster Hyman Roth, played by famed acting coach Lee Strasberg.

Michael at the gambling tables in Nevada, where the Corleone family has relocated.

series of vignettes: Jewish gangster Hyman Roth (Lee Strasberg), who orchestrated the unsuccessful hit on Michael at Lake Tahoe, is murdered at the airport as he talks to reporters; Frankie slashes his wrists in the bathtub while in protective custody; and—best of all—Fredo is shot in a rowboat on the quiet lake while Pacino watches sorrowfully but determinedly from the shore.

Clad in ascot and with slicked-back hair, Pacino plays with restraint and ever-present menace, icy, smooth, with a poker-player, butter-wouldn't-melt-in-his-mouth expression. The trouble is, Pacino isn't really given a *character* to play, as Michael Corleone is more of an icon in *The Godfather, Part II* than a fully realized human being. Worse, Pacino at times underplays too much and talks too low and in an enervated fashion that borders on somnambulism. Perhaps he felt that the once-decent Michael Corleone would be suffering a deep depression because of all the vile actions he must undertake, with those enervating results. If so, Pacino was giving the material too much credit and subjecting it to too much analysis. Besides,

one suspects that Michael Corleone, like his father before him, was never *that* bothered by anything he did.

Still, Pacino has more than his share of impressive sequences, such as when he confronts his brother Fredo over his betrayal, kisses him full on the lips, and says, "I know it was you, Fredo. You broke my heart. *You broke my heart.*" He registers a quivering, quiet intensity during a confrontation with Kay, when she tells him she had an abortion without his knowledge. One of Pacino's best scenes is an ironic 1941 flashback that shows him and the other members of the Corleone family at the dinner table. While his slimeball relatives talk about avoiding the post–Pearl Harbor draft, Michael calmly announces that he has enlisted in the marines. What a tragedy that the only heroic individual in the Corleone family should ultimately choose a path so corrupt and debasing.

As for the famous Pacino blasts? Well, Pacino's underplaying in this, as in the original *Godfather,* keeps the blasts to a minimum and reduces their intensity, but he does explode more than once, screaming at

Michael looks affectionately at the godfather.

At a Senate investigation into the Mafia, Michael and his lawyer Tom Hagen (Robert Duvall) deny all.

Kay (after hitting her), "*You won't take my children!*" He also gives Robert Duvall a miniblast when the latter tries to tell him the news of Kay's "miscarriage." "Can't you give me a straight answer? *Was it a boy?*" The best blast occurs when Michael confronts turncoat Frankie after being nearly riddled with bullets in his own bedroom. He dances about the man very quietly, deceptively, then bursts out with "*In my home!*" (Only a murderous mafioso could be so filled with righteous indignation.)

The Godfather, Part II is packed with talented supporting players, but three deserve special mention. Talia Shire (Coppola's sister) proves that it wasn't mere nepotism that got her the coveted role of sister Connie. Whether flaunting her gigolo boyfriend (Troy Donahue) and dissipated lifestyle in Michael's face or telling him she forgives him for the murder of her husband ("You were being strong for the family like Papa was"), she gets across her rather desperate, pathetic character very tellingly. Celebrated acting coach Lee Strasberg had never appeared in a film

before being cast as the genteel (but not Gentile) gangster Hyman Roth; quietly telling lies to Michael as he watches TV or chairing a meeting of mobsters in Havana, he proves that during all those years of teaching he knew what he was talking about. John Cazale, as Fredo, gives a very strong performance and etches a memorable portrait of the screw-up Corleone brother who has been passed over as Michael makes it to the top. "I want *respect,*" he tells Pacino. Any actor who can make a loser like Fredo seem sympathetic deserves respect, all right. Unfortunately, Shire and Strasberg were nominated for supporting Oscars, while Cazale—like Fredo—was overlooked.

Michael V. Gazzo also got a supporting Oscar nomination for playing the gravel-voiced, whining turncoat Frankie. Gazzo is good, but one suspects this is an actor of decidedly limited range whose whole career has been playing one variation of Frankie after another. The role of Kay has practically been reduced to a walk-on, and this time Diane Keaton isn't very good. During the Senate hearings on the Mafia, one of the senators is played (adequately) by Roger Corman, who produced some of Coppola's earliest features and gave him a start in the business.

Pacino was nominated for Best Actor and De Niro for Best Supporting Actor; this time the screen father won out over his "son." Although De Niro became a star with *The Godfather, Part II* and is fine in the role, his performance is hardly Oscar-worthy. (Neither is Pacino's, for that matter.) But it was a "big" picture, and the academy loves big pictures and the actors in them. The movie also won Oscars for Best Picture, Best Screenplay, Best Score, and Best Director. Practically a solid sweep.

Not even nominated were production designer Dean Tavoularis, who provided an excellent re-creation of 1917 Little Italy, teeming with merchants, wagons, and children, and cinematographer Gordon Willis, who contributed some sumptuous shots of beautiful Sicilian settings, not to mention New York and Lake Tahoe.

Despite the accolades, there are problems with *The Godfather, Part II*. The script for the 1950s story line is too diffuse, moving in too many directions, and hasn't a strong enough plot. The whole mid-film business with the gangsters and unstable political situation in Cuba is convoluted and tiresome and belongs in a different picture. Running over three hours, the movie is often quite slow-paced. It is not as strong or as entertaining as the original film.

Michael forgives straying brother Fredo (John Cazale) but has him killed, anyway.

Al Pacino exudes charm as Michael Corleone.

81

There is no question that the Mafia is romanticized a bit too much in *The Godfather, Part II.* Virtually all of the adversaries of the Corleone family are reptiles. (But surely the Mafia kills innocents once in a while?) Young Vito Corleone's victims are two slimy dons, one who rides herd over Little Italy and another who kills women and children with hardly a backward glance. Once Vito is set up as the new don in New York, his first act is to keep a poor, helpless widow from being thrown out onto the street! Decades later, the murder of Connie's husband is minimized because he was a creep and a wife beater. It's as if the film were saying: "These guys are good guys. They were victims, too. They only kill people who deserve it." The real-life Mafia is hardly so benign.

The question persists: Why do so many talented Italian-American filmmakers and actors—the best of their community—insist on making motion pictures that celebrate the activities of the *worst* of their community?

The saga of the Corleone family wasn't over, but Al Pacino had many other projects before it was through.

Master of all he surveys? Not quite. His wife has left him. Al Pacino as Michael Corleone.

82

DOG DAY AFTERNOON

Warner Brothers, 1975

Producers, Martin Bregman and Martin Elfand; director, Sidney Lumet; director of photography, Victor J. Kemper; editor, Dede Allen; screenplay, Frank Pierson; associate producer, Robert Greenhut; art director, Burtt Harris; production designer, Charles Bailey; costume designer, Anna Hill Johnstone. Running time: 130 min.

CAST

Al Pacino (*Sonny Wortzik*); John Cazale (*Sal*); Chris Sarandon (*Leon*); Susan Peretz (*Angie*); Judith Malina (*Mother*); Charles Durning (*Detective Moretti*); Penelope Allen (*Sylvia*); Sully Boyar (*Mulvaney*); James Broderick (*Sheldon*); Lance Henriksen (*Murphy*); Dick Anthony Williams (*Limo Driver*); Carol Kane (*Jenny*); John Marriot (*Howard*); Sandra Kazan (*Deborah*); Gary Springer (*Stevie*); Beulah Garrick (*Margaret*); Marcia Jean Kurtz (*Miriam*); Amy Levitt (*Maria*).

Al Pacino as Sonny Wortzik, the world's worst bank robber, in *Dog Day Afternoon*.

One of the zaniest—and most pathetic—bank-robbery attempts of all time took place on August 22, 1972, in Brooklyn, New York. So bizarre were aspects of this real-life occurrence that it is easy to see why the subject matter proved irresistible to filmmakers. The result was *Dog Day Afternoon* (as in, presumably, every dog has his day or, in this case, a hot August afternoon and part of the evening).

The "dog" was "Sonny Wortzik" (Al Pacino)—a variation of the man's real name—and a bigger loser it would be hard to find. The bank holdup he plans with two colleagues goes awry right from the start. First, one of the robbers chickens out immediately after Sonny makes his move and has to be let out of the bank. "Don't take the car!" Sonny tells him, know-

83

Sal (John Cazale) and Sonny (Pacino) get ready to stick up the bank.

supposedly have a plane ready to take the two desperadoes to Algeria. "There's a Howard Johnson's there," Sonny explains. But before they can board the plane, Sal is shot in the forehead by a Federal Bureau of Investigations (FBI) man, and Sonny is taken into custody. His sentence: twenty years in a federal penitentiary.

At first, Pacino, who is not a nerd, as Sonny is, seems miscast. But he manages to play a dork dynamically without making the character seem *less* of one. Although far more attractive than the real Sonny, Pacino does an excellent imitation of him, getting across his essential *schlumpiness,* the puppylike, shuffling manner, and the incipient craziness lying just below the surface. The voice is also perfect, reeking of Brooklyn and hinting of vulnerabilities that Sonny tries to dis-

ing he'll need it for a getaway. "How'll I get home?" whines the boy, Stevie (Gary Springer). "Take the subway," Sonny tells him.

Then it turns out that most of the money in the bank was picked up earlier in the day and only $1,100 is left in the vault. Sonny lights a fire in a garbage can, and the smoke attracts the attention of a shopkeeper and then the police. Before Sonny and his remaining colleague, Sal (John Cazale), can make their getaway, they are surrounded by 250 cops. Drawn into hostage negotiations with a detective, Moretti (Charles Durning), Sonny says he wants to talk to his wife, but the wife they bring is not his spouse, Angie (Susan Peretz), but a male lover whom Sonny married in a special gay ceremony. "Leon" (Chris Sarandon), fresh from Bellevue, needs a sex-change operation, which Sonny apparently was planning to finance with the proceeds from the robbery.

Sonny, Sal, and their comparatively friendly hostages set off in a limo to the airport, where the police

An "amiable" Sonny instructs the tellers to line up while the manager goes to get the money.

guise with nervous, angry chatter and vocal outbursts, such as when he yells at Durning—whom he feels is trying to put one over on him—"Kiss me! When I'm being fucked, I like to be kissed!" He delivers a mini–Pacino blast to his chatterbox wife. "Will you shut up and *just listen to me!*"

Pacino had mixed emotions about playing a major gay (or bisexual) lead in a popular (as opposed to "art") film, which had really not been done before. To his credit, he resists camping it up or stereotyping the character. In real life, Sonny may have been a nerd, but he was not a lisping, limp-wristed queen, and Pacino was right not to play him that way.

Pacino is matched in brilliance by Chris Sarandon as his "lover," who really doesn't want any part of him. Leon, who *is* a queen, holds one hand perpetually up

Sal keeps watch over the bank tellers with his weapon in hand.

to his neck as if to register his disbelief that any of this can be happening. Leon likes how he's treated in Bellevue but has some doubts. "They say you're crazy, and right away they stick somethin' in ya arm, and pretty soon you're sleepin'. How can you get *un*crazy when ya sleepin' all the time?" Leon's sense of humor is his saving grace. "(Sonny's) mother and father together are like a bad car wreck."

The highlight of the picture is Sonny's phone conversation with Leon; the two principal actors improvised much of their dialogue, according to Sidney Lumet. When Sonny asks Leon to accompany him on

85

Detective Moretti (Charles Durning) tries to reason with Sonny.

his flight out of the country, Leon snaps: "I've been tryin' to get away from you for six months, and I'm gonna go with you on a *plane trip*?" Then he asks, "Where are ya goin'?" Sonny is unmoved by Leon's whining. "Sal thinks Wyoming is a country. He doesn't know where it is. You think you got problems? I'm with a guy who doesn't know where Wyoming is!"

Speaking of Sal, he's very well played by John Cazale, who had also supported Pacino in *The Godfather* films. The role of Sal is not as showy as that of Fredo Corleone—Cazale actually hasn't much to do and is saddled with an impossible, ambiguous part—but he plays it with quiet effectiveness and restrained intensity. The look on Cazale's face as he sits in the backseat of the limo at the airport seems to suggest that Sal senses the approach of his own death moments later. (Sadly, Cazale himself would be dead of bone cancer within three years.)

Cazale also has a few good moments when Sal hears a news report claiming that "two homosexuals" have robbed the First Brooklyn Savings Bank. "But *I'm* not a homosexual" he says in distress. When an FBI agent comes into the bank to check on the hostages, Sal says to him, "Tell the TV to stop sayin' there's two homosexuals in here." Sal doesn't care if people know he's a bank robber, but he doesn't want anyone to think he's gay.

Pacino, Sarandon, and Cazale were all nominated

Sonny tells Detective Moretti where he can go and then some.

Sonny waves to his fan club outside the bank as head teller Sylvia (Penelope Allen) kibitzes.

Detective Moretti makes another stab at reasoning with the unreasonable Sonny Wortzik.

Sonny's mother pleads with him to stop this foolishness.

for Oscars, as were the picture and Lumet (who turned in one of his better directorial efforts). Only screenwriter Frank Pierson brought home the coveted statue, however.

Another highlight is Sonny's phone conversation with spouse Angie, who is convinced she is the cause of Sonny's falling for Leon. "I know I let myself get fat," she says. Susan Peretz manages to make Angie touching beneath the farcical exterior. For her part, Sonny's mother (Judith Malina) agrees with her daughter-in-law: "You wouldn't need Leon if Angie were treating you right," she avers in a hilarious encounter with her nebbish son on the sidewalk outside the bank as hundreds of cops, spectators, and media people watch Sonny trying to deal with his well-meaning, if kvetching, mother. Malina makes the most of her brief bit, as does Gary Springer, as Stevie, the friend who bolts from the bank at the beginning of the picture.

Also in the cast was Pacino's old friend Penny (now

billed "Penelope") Allen, as the chief teller Sylvia. Allen, who was wonderful in *Scarecrow*, has more to do in *Dog Day Afternoon* but fewer *dramatic* scenes (nothing along the lines of her phone conversation with Lion in *Scarecrow*). Still, Allen has a breezy way with the material. Witness her evocative delivery of "So you rob a bank, but you keep your body pure" to health advocate Sal, who has chided her for lighting a cigarette. Charles Durning's contribution as Moretti cannot be underestimated, and James Broderick and Lance Henriksen are also fine as FBI agents who finally put a stop to the nonsense. Dick Anthony Williams as the limo driver (who is also a cop) is also fun as he chortles to Sonny, "You gonna shoot, aim for white meat."

Although talky, the film has a few spurts of excitement, such as when Sonny nearly causes a riot by throwing money into the crowd outside the bank. The excellent opening montage of New Yorkers at work and play, its beaches, sidewalks, bridges, and traffic, winds up with a striking, ominous—and prescient— shot of a cemetery with the New York skyline in the background. Editor Dede Allen really shows her stuff with a cinematic sequence showing cops trying to enter the bank through the back of the building. Bits with the security guard being mistaken for one of the bank robbers, a pizza delivery boy who carries on like a star when he hands the pizzas to Sonny, and a hostage's Italian boyfriend who pounces on Sonny and is carted away by the cops for his trouble (*he's treated far more roughly than Sonny is!*) also compen-

Sonny attempts to restrain a panicking Sylvia (Penny Allen).

Sal sits in back of the limo with teller Jenny (Carol Kane) moments before his death.

89

sate for the film's slower stretches. The climactic motorcade to the airport is also well handled, with crowds alternately rooting the robbers on or trying to smash the windows of the limo with bottles.

Dog Day Afternoon was made at a time when the country was more naive about the crime situation, when it was still possible to laugh at bungling bank robbers. Sonny tells Sal that he doesn't mean it when he threatens to "throw out the bodies of the hostages," but early in the picture he tells Stevie, the recalcitrant robber, to "take his head off!" if the security guard makes a move (which prompts Stevie to bolt from the bank). Whatever Sonny's nature, Sal seems more than capable of killing someone. If no one but Sal died, it may have been due more to luck than Sonny's alleged compassion. When Sonny expresses concern over the bank manager's diabetes, the manager says: "I wish you had never come into this bank. Don't try to act like you're some angel of human kindness!"

There was a lot of antiauthority feeling in the seventies, and this was carried over to the police, who are booed by the crowds outside the bank when Sonny screams, "Attica! Attica!" When it is discovered that Sonny has a male lover, the "lunatic fringe" of the gay community (hardly its more sensible, mainstream members) also show up to cheer Sonny on. (None of these nitwits, however—gay or straight—offers to take the place of one of the hostages in the bank!) But Sonny isn't an anti-Establishment "hero"; he's a loser with a wife and kids on welfare who seeks money not to help his family but his "lover," who wants no part of him.

To their credit, the filmmakers *aren't* saying that Sonny is a hero; they are only documenting the moronic reactions of the crowd. But the comic aspects of his actions serve to minimize the actuality of what he's doing, as well as the sheer *terror* that must have been felt by the bank tellers. We're even manipulated into feeling bad for the creepy Sal when he's killed by the FBI (Moral: If you don't want to get shot by the cops, don't commit crimes.)

Dog Day Afternoon was probably as upsetting to the Polish-American Anti-Defamation League as it was to some gays, but it is memorable as a generally funny burlesque show and slice of outré New York life—and for Pacino's excellent performance.

After his sex-change operation ("Leon Schermer is now a woman and living in New York" reads an end-credit title), the real Leon changed his name to "Liz Eden." Liz danced topless at the Hungry Hilda on Eighth Avenue for a while, then tried to become one of the endless New Yorkers famous for being famous, but nobody cared. She, like Sonny, has faded into well-deserved obscurity.

BOBBY DEERFIELD

Warner Brothers/Columbia Pictures, 1977

Executive producer, John Foreman; producer, Sydney Pollack; director, Pollack; director of photography, Henri Decaë; editor, Fredric Steinkamp; screenplay, Alvin Sargent; based on *Heaven Has No Favorites* by Erich Maria Remarque; music, Dave Grusin; production designer, Stephen Grimes. Running time: 123 min.

CAST

Al Pacino (*Bobby Deerfield*); Marthe Keller (*Lillian*); Walter McGinn (Leonard); Stephan Meldegg (*Karl Holzman*); Anny Duperey (*Lydia*); Romolo Valli (*Uncle Luigi*); Norm Nielsen (*the Magician*); Jaime Sanchez (*Delvecchio*); Mickey Knox, Dorothy James (*Tourists*).

Bobby Deerfield was Al Pacino's eighth picture and the first of his that wasn't a particularly good movie. The movie's intentions may have been admirable, but its execution faltered. Some critics felt *Bobby Deerfield* was Pacino's certified turkey; it is actually only one of two or three disappointing films in a career of mostly hits instead of misses. *Bobby Deerfield* isn't a complete stinker—but close.

Pacino plays a racing driver, Bobby Deerfield, whose friend has just died in an accident. Bobby

Pacino gives his patented brooding intensity a workout as Bobby Deerfield.

wonders what caused the accident—something on the track, perhaps?—and heads for a clinic where Karl Holzman, another racer-friend, is recuperating. In the dining room an enigmatic young lady at the next table asks to borrow the butter and begins a conversation with Bobby. She is another patient, named Lillian (Marthe Keller).

Lillian is insolent and presumptuous, borderline rude and insulting, yet oddly engaging. Bobby agrees to give her a ride home from the clinic. The two begin an affair, and Bobby learns that Lillian is dying of an unspecified illness. After a few days together, Lillian asks Bobby to take her back to the clinic. ("I was thinking about your friend Holzman. I think I would

like to go back—to see how he is.") Lillian dies while at the clinic, and Bobby goes on with his life.

Bobby Deerfield presents a "kinder, gentler" Al Pacino than had been seen in previous pictures, "Lion" in *Scarecrow* notwithstanding. Alvin Sargent's screenplay doesn't tell us much about Bobby—or Lillian, for that matter—but Pacino does the best he can with the material. Pacino is never somnambulistic, as he sometimes is in *The Godfather, Part II,* just more low-key and subdued. Even the sweet character of Lion had a little more of an edge to him (with a nervous breakdown to boot). Deerfield may have come from Newark, New Jersey, but he's as suave and polished as the European surroundings.

Pacino's acting cannot be faulted. He has an expert, natural reaction when he learns from his French girlfriend, Lydia, what she already heard through the grapevine, that Lillian is dying. Later on, as Lillian lies in her bed in the clinic singing, her death is mirrored only in Pacino's eyes as her singing stops, the camera fixed on Bobby's face. Pacino underplays beautifully.

At one point, Pacino is allowed to work up some fire (if not quite a blast) as he confronts Keller in a big field where she is waiting to take off in a hot-air balloon. Deerfield is exasperated at Lillian's attitude and at the way she left him in the morning without saying where she was going. But Lillian refuses to behave like a typical dying person. When she leaves

Things get hot for Pacino when his car catches fire.

When Pacino's friend is killed in a car wreck, his pit mechanic (Jaime Sanchez) tries to restrain him.

the clinic early, the nurse says, "Madame—the rules?" to which Lillian replies, "No rules. I come to death on my own terms."

Trying to make Lillian laugh at one point, Bobby/Pacino launches into one of the most god-awful impersonations of Mae West ever recorded on camera. (Pacino should stick to Boris Karloff, whom he did pretty well in *Scarecrow*.) Of course, Bobby's impression isn't supposed to be very good.

Marthe Keller makes a very chic—if, at times,

tacky—Camille. Lillian tells Bobby that she thinks racing is boring and that a racing car "is only an extension of a man's penis." She asks Bobby, "Are you a homo?" and wonders if there are any homos in New Jersey. Passing through a tunnel in Bobby's car, she screams out loud. She is a scared, defiant woman-child saying whatever comes into her mind, regardless of its effect. It's as if she feels that the fact that she's dying gives her the right to say or do anything.

Marthe Keller is adept at revealing the surface of

93

Deerfield relaxes between races.

her character but lacks the talent to show us the vulnerability underneath. In a previous decade Margaret Sullavan (who did appear in two adaptations of Erich Maria Remarque novels) would have been cast in the role and would have been much better, delineating both Lillian's desperate obnoxiousness and the sad, frightened, lonely quality beneath.

While Keller may not have overly impressed the critics, she did make an impression on Pacino, who took her for his lover and moved her into his apartment back in New York City. Keller's American film career never really took off, however (the disappointing grosses of *Bobby Deerfield*, after appearances in such blockbusters as *Marathon Man* and *Black Sunday*, couldn't have helped); she was a limited performer and perhaps too Germanic to appeal to American audiences, the (more talented) Marlene Dietrich notwithstanding.

One actor in *Bobby Deerfield* who was closer to the mark was Walter McGinn, who does a nice job as Bobby's brother Leonard. Pacino and McGinn help sustain the tension in a restaurant encounter between brothers in which Leonard—who has a "safer," if less glamorous, job in the printing business—chastises Bobby for not taking time to see their mother (an alcoholic). McGinn gets across the brother's bitterness; Leonard is saddled with a wife, three kids, and a mother-in-law and, in addition, has to attend to the family responsibilities all by himself, while footloose Bobby indulges in an irresponsible lifestyle. Yet Leonard has made his choices and must live with them. (Ironically, McGinn was killed in an automobile accident only a few months after the film was released.) Anny Duperey and Romolo Valli are also notable as, respectively, Bobby's appealing French girlfriend, Lydia, and Lillian's uncle Luigi, with whom Lillian lives.

The picture is not without its worthwhile moments, such as a charming scene in a nightspot when Bobby and Lillian ask the magician who has just performed to give away his secrets. "It's magic," he insists. An oddly touching moment (one that some viewers giggle at) occurs when Bobby takes pieces of Lily's hair that have fallen out onto the pillow and pointlessly tries to place them back on her head. Yet it bespeaks tenderness and confusion and somehow works. By far the best scene is a poignant bit when a couple of middle-aged tourists, husband and wife, ask Bobby to

Lillian (Marthe Keller) has an earnest chat with her new lover, Bobby Deerfield.

Deerfield is ready to take off for another spin around the track.

Pacino as smooth, urbane Bobby Deerfield.

take their picture and then snap one of Bobby and Lillian. They ask for an address where they can send it. All the while it is apparent to us and to the young lovers that Lillian will probably be dead before they ever receive it. (We see a shot of the snapshot at the end of the film.) For a few moments you're almost fooled into thinking you're seeing a better picture than *Bobby Deerfield* really is.

What went wrong with *Bobby Deerfield*? Sydney Pollack's direction is perfectly fluid; the acting is acceptable (and in the case of Pacino and some others even better than that); Henri Decaë's cinematography, with

Bobby is all decked out and ready to race.

A haunted Deerfield, who now knows his lover is dying, is obsessed with how little time they have.

Bobby and Lillian stop for a rest while sightseeing.

98

Lydia (Anny Duperey), Bobby's French girlfriend, isn't happy over the time he's spending with Lillian.

Director Sydney Pollack
(*left*) gives instruction to
his stars Pacino and Keller
in the hot-air balloon
scene.

Marthe Keller and Al Pacino became lovers in real life; their relationship did not last.

its striking shots of Paris and Florence and, in particular, a flight of hot-air balloons (the balloons look like mammoth, bloated sailboats in the sky), is excellent; and Dave Grusin's music, with its Spanish guitars and European flavor, is often lovely.

The trouble is that the source material, Erich Maria Remarque's novel *Heaven Has No Favorites,* is essentially a European product, and a period piece at that. Updated and made by (mostly) Americans, with an insufficient script (the novel may not have been a good bet for film adaptation), the results were less than felicitous. *Bobby Deerfield* was an attempt to make an *English-language* European film, but Sydney Pollack is no Fellini. The movie is an odd, moody hybrid that never quite soars. The enigmatic main characters are of no help. The picture should have been a powerful study of loneliness, but it isn't.

Still, it has its evocative moments, such as when Lillian tells Bobby the story of her father's death, how he keeled over suddenly on the beach and fell on top of a child. "It was like, in dying, he gave birth to the child, like an egg."

But all the (at times) heavy-handed death symbolism isn't enough to save *Bobby Deerfield,* which had many Pacino fans wishing it had been an offer Pacino could have refused.

A sensitive portrait of Al Pacino as Bobby Deerfield.

Pacino had one of his best roles as the passionate Arthur Kirkland.

. . . AND JUSTICE FOR ALL

Columbia, 1979

Executive producer, Joe Wizen; producers, Norman Jewison and Patrick Palmer; director, Norman Jewison; director of photography, Victor J. Kemper; aerial photography, Frank Holgate; editor, John F. Burnett, A.C.E.; screenplay, Valerie Curtin and Barry Levinson; music, Dave Grusin; production designer, Richard MacDonald; costume designer, Ruth Myers. Running time: 120 min.

CAST

Al Pacino (*Arthur Kirkland*); Jack Warden (*Judge Rayford*); John Forsythe (*Judge Fleming*); Lee Strasberg (*Grandpa Sam*); Jeffrey Tambor (*Jay Porter*); Christine Lahti (*Gail Packer*); Dominic Chianese (*Carl Travers*); Thomas Waites (*Jeff McCullough*); Robert Christian (*Ralph Agee*); Craig T. Nelson (*Frank Bowers*); Stephen Blackmore (*Robert Winkle*); Charles Siebert (*Kane*); Keith Andes (*Marvin Bates*); Sam Levene (*Arnie*); Teri Wootten (*Leah Shephard*); Larry Bryggman (*Warren Fresnell*).

Baltimore lawyer Arthur Kirkland (Al Pacino) is being kept very busy. His nemesis, Judge Henry Fleming (John Forsythe) has had him thrown in jail for contempt of court. A wealthy client is trapped in his car with a hooker after an accident. Another client—

whose arrest was due to a mistaken identity—must remain in jail because the statute of limitations has run out on presenting new evidence. Kirkland's partner suffers a breakdown and must be carted away, with Kirkland at his side, meaning a disinterested associate has to stand in for the sentencing of a transvestite. When the associate muffs the whole thing, the client commits suicide when he learns he has to go to jail.

To cap it all, Judge Fleming is accused of raping, beating, and sodomizing a young lady and chooses Arthur for his lawyer. Arthur knows this is a case that can make or break a reputation, but when he learns Judge Fleming is guilty, he goes berserk in the courtroom and delivers a speech condemning the hypocritical Fleming, to all intents and purposes destroying his own career in the process.

Pacino again received an Academy Award nomination for Best Actor for . . . *and Justice for All*; it is one of his most winning performances, with the actor at his most assured, confident, and charismatic. Arthur Kirkland is one of Pacino's most likable creations. Whether he is quietly but firmly telling off an ethics committee or telling a recalcitrant client not to "bullshit" him, you're with him all the way. . . .*and Justice for All* gives Pacino plenty of opportunities to deliver

his patented blasts, but he is also excellent in the "smaller" scenes, such as when he meets his grandfather's elderly lady friend and displays a polite, realistic awkwardness.

Humor isn't always Pacino's forte, but he's very funny when Judge Rayford (Jack Warden), a certified eccentric, takes him for a helicopter ride and tells him he might not have enough fuel to get back. Pacino evinces convincing queasiness and distress, and then hilarious hysteria, as the copter plummets into the bay and the two are nearly killed. Sitting in a coffee shop later, chattering, and with a blanket thrown over him, his barely restrained fury at Warden is delightful.

Pacino's climactic speech to the jury is "showy" in the best sense of the word, filled with riveting pyrotechnics, as if Pacino knew the only way to make the contrived scene work was to play it for all it was worth. He builds up slowly but forcefully to the Pacino blast, then points to Judge Fleming and screams: *That man should go right to fuckin' jail!"*

But Pacino's finest moment occurs after his associate, Warren (Larry Bryggman), blows it in court and the transvestite-client kills himself rather than go to jail, which Pacino had promised him would not happen. First Pacino smashes the windows of Warren's

Kirkland discusses the finer points of law while in bed with girlfriend Gail (Christine Lahti).

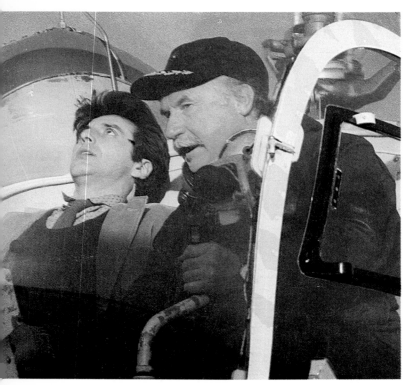

Arthur has a near-death experience while flying in a helicopter with the zany Judge Rayford (Jack Warden).

car as it halts on its way out of the parking garage. He continues battering the automobile as Warren does his best to calm him down. Finally, Warren gets out of the car to talk to him after making Pacino promise to reign himself in. Pacino plays the scene with heartbreaking sincerity, going from fury, righteous anger, and passion to grief and simple *com*passion: "Don't you *care*?" he says to Warren. "They're just people— *don't you care*?" It is one of the strongest scenes Pacino has ever played and proof positive that he is one of our most passionate and poignant actors.

Others in the cast also give fine performances, such as John Forsythe as the reptilian Judge Fleming, who sits in court with a smug, calm demeanor as if only he is allowed to be above the law regardless of what atrocities he has committed. Jack Warden scores, as expected, as the unconventional judge who eats his lunch on a ledge outside his window several stories up, attempts suicide every so often for the hell of it, and bets his (and his passengers') lives on whether or not his copter can make it back on however little fuel remains. Lee Strasberg essays a very different part from his mobster in *The Godfather, Part II* as Pacino's

wise, warm, but hopelessly senile grandfather, but is just as strong and convincing. Talented actress Christine Lahti, however, is pretty much wasted as Gail Packer, with whom Kirkland has a relationship of sorts.

The usually reliable Jeffrey Tambor, as Kirkland's partner, Jay Porter, seems a bit off in . . . *and Justice for All,* possibly because of the way his role is written. Porter's problems begin when a murderer he has gotten off murders again. We're asked to believe that a slick lawyer who would have no problem defending someone he knows to be guilty of a heinous murder (all that about everyone, even the guilty, having a right to a fair trial notwithstanding) would suffer a nervous breakdown because his client has murdered again. But if the lawyer didn't care about the first victim, why the second? While it might be believable that Porter would feel some slight guilt, it isn't believable that he would shave his head as a reaction to his internal distress or grab stacks of plates from the cafeteria and fling them at all and sundry who walk down the hall toward his office in the courthouse.

At least this situation makes for a lively sequence, with Warden running interference as he and Pacino hurl themselves down the corridor dodging missiles as Tambor screams, plates smash on walls and floor, and Pacino makes a desperate bid to stop and control his partner before the police can make their move. Like a lot of scenes in this picture, it *plays* without ever being convincing.

The casting of some of the smaller parts is particularly good, such as Robert Christian as the pathetic drag queen who has been arrested for participating in a holdup of a taxi driver, and Thomas Waites, who makes the most of the kid incarcerated simply because he was mistaken for somebody else. Dominic Chianese is fun as Pacino's big-bucks, womanizing client who says to a rescue worker trying to cut him out of a smashed-up automobile: "Can't you see I'm on the [car] phone?" Sam Levene as grandpa's buddy and Keith Andes as Bates, Judge Fleming's colleague, are also notable.

But as entertaining and well acted as . . . *and Justice for All* may be, it almost sinks under its contrivances. And the script has too many melodramatic scenes in a row: Tambor goes berserk, the transvestite commits suicide, the wrong-identity client also loses it, ties up two guards, and winds up shot to death by the police—all of this happens within half an hour, it seems.

Arthur Kirkland gets ready for his day in court.

Judge Rayford and Arthur try their best to restrain Arthur's suddenly demented law partner, Jay (Jeffrey Tambor).

Worse still, much of the screenplay asks us to accept too much. Forsythe *admits* his guilt to Pacino, which he would *never* have done. Pacino (earlier) assumes that Forsythe is guilty simply because someone gives him sleazy pictures showing Fleming with a hooker. Kirkland is mad at Fleming because the judge refuses to look at new evidence which might free the wrong-identity client, but it takes weeks for him to say to the judge that he'll represent him *if* he agrees to look at the new evidence. Why didn't Kirkland make this point the *first* time Fleming asks him to be his lawyer?

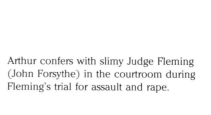

Arthur confers with slimy Judge Fleming (John Forsythe) in the courtroom during Fleming's trial for assault and rape.

The whole business with Tambor's guilt and breakdown might have been believable if it had been developed properly *in another picture*. And while Kirkland's telling the jury in righteous outrage that his client Fleming is guilty and should go to jail is a hell of a lot of fun, it doesn't make a lick of sense. Pacino is throwing his career away (what client, guilty or innocent, would want this loon for a lawyer?), and Fleming will simply be given a new trial and a more amenable solicitor. For all Kirkland's indignation and integrity, *nothing has been gained*. Everyone knows that Fleming and Kirkland hate each other, so the latter's outburst won't even be taken that seriously (and it certainly doesn't mean that Fleming will be convicted). In its effort to be a "feel good" movie, *. . . and Justice for All* sacrifices veracity.

"*Let* criminals create their own hellhole," says Judge Fleming. "What we need is *un*just punishment. Is bringing Johnny Cash into prison to sing songs going to rehabilitate anyone?" The judge actually makes some excellent points, but the script's somewhat "bleeding heart" slant ensures that the audience won't take them

seriously because Fleming is a hypocrite, a ranter, and never listens to what is actually being said by Kirkland (for instance, that his wrong-identity client is innocent). We're asked to cry for the drag queen who kills himself but not to feel anything for the hardworking cabdriver he helped rob.

Still, . . . *and Justice for All* tries to be fair and does get across the insanity of the "justice" system. One scene has a public defender pleading with an assistant D.A. to reduce his client's sentence because he's *afraid* to tell him he'll have to spend a year in jail. A criminal who grabbed an elderly woman's purse and *beat her* in all sincerity blames the victim because he "meant no harm . . . she shoulda let go." The picture is consistently flavorful and colorful and fast-paced, even if Norman Jewison's unobtrusive direction doesn't really do much for the film.

Al Pacino deserves high marks for triumphing over an impossible script and coming out on top, after all.

Now it's Arthur's turn to be restrained when he tells the whole court that his client, Fleming, belongs in jail.

CRUISING

Lorimar, 1980

Producer, Jerry Weintraub; director, William Friedkin. director of photography, James Contner; editor, Bud Smith; screenplay, Friedkin; based on the novel by Gerald Walker; music, Jack Nitzsche; art director, Edward Pisoni; production designer, Bruce Weintraub; costume designer, Robert de Mora. Running time: 106 min.

CAST

Al Pacino (*Steve Burns*); Paul Sorvino (*Captain Edelson*); Karen Allen (*Nancy*); Don Scardino (*Ted Bailey*); Allan Miller (*Chief of Detectives*); Jay Acovone (*Skip Lee*); Richard Cox (*Stuart Richards*); Arnaldo Santana (*Loren Luka*); James Remar (*Greg*); Joe Spinell (*DeSimone*); Edward O'Neil (*Detective Schreiber*); Powers Boothe (*Hanky Salesman*); James Sutorius (*Voice of Jack*).

Why did Al Pacino want to do *Cruising*? Regardless of its controversial aspects, the script offered Pacino very few dramatic possibilities and not even a great deal of dialogue. His role is primarily a passive one: He goes from place to place studying, watching, occasionally reacting. The true mystery of the film is why he thought it would be a good project for him.

Steve is ready to party—and catch a killer.

Cruising began life as a penny-dreadful thriller by former *New York Times* editor Gerald Walker. The novel deals with a cop who goes undercover to catch a serial killer of gay men. The killer, a college student, goes berserk in a bathhouse, severing men's penises and placing them in their mouths. The student's spree of violence is ended, but it is suggested that the whole business will start all over again when the cop kills a man with whom he has his first homosexual experience.

Walker felt that he had exposed the roots of homophobia: His killers are murdering their repressed homosexual natures. But homophobia, like all prejudice, has a variety of causes, from inferiority complexes to ignorance to societal and religious pressures. Walker compared his novel to the Broadway show *Bent*—which detailed the persecution of homosexuals during the Nazi regime—ignoring the fact that the play was a serious work of theater and of artistic merit, while his novel was an indifferently written potboiler devoid of much depth or characterization. (This same problem was carried over to the film.)

Brian De Palma, with whom Pacino would work on *Scarface* and *Carlito's Way*, was first interested in filming *Cruising*, but his script was very different from the one penned by eventual director William Friedkin. De Palma's killer is not a repressed homosexual but a failed actor who videotapes his murders (as does the killer in Michael Powell's *Peeping Tom*) and kills a woman at one point just to throw the police off his

Once the assignment starts, Steve has precious little time to spend with his girlfriend Nancy (Karen Allen).

Steve has a friendly chat with his likable neighbor, Ted (Don Scardino).

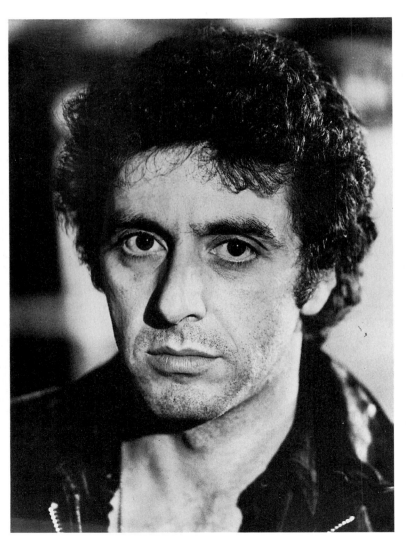

Pacino as Steve Burns, undercover cop, in *Cruising*.

111

Decked out in hot leather, Steve heads out to his first gay bar.

track. (This particular murder became the elevator razor-slashing of Angie Dickinson in De Palma's *Dressed to Kill*.)

Director William Friedkin, famous for *The Exorcist* (1973) and *French Connection* (1971), hadn't had a hit in years—and needed one. For his part, Pacino had only made two pictures in the five years since *Dog Day Afternoon*, and neither of them had done that well at the box office. Both men undoubtedly felt that an unusual, graphic shocker like *Cruising* would stir up a lot of controversy, get plenty of advance press, and emerge a hit. They were mistaken.

The police find a human arm in the river and assume its from the latest victim of a killer who preys on homosexuals. Steven Burns (Al Pacino), a young police officer, is chosen to go undercover in the gay community because of his strong resemblance to the other victims. Steve finds himself somewhat mesmerized by the hedonistic, sensual goings-on in the gay S and M hangouts he must frequent as part of his investigation. He tells his captain it's too much for him, but the superior officer insists he remain on the case. After a series of killings, the trail leads to Stuart Richards (Richard Cox), a student at Columbia University. Richards and Burns square off in a tense Central Park encounter, with Burns the victor. After Richards's

Pacino "gets down" on the dance floor and boogies with the gay guys.

arrest, Burns's gay neighbor Ted Bailey (Don Scardino) is found murdered. When the captain learns that Steve was living just down the hall from the victim, he mutters, "Oh, my God."

Affecting a curlier, fluffier hairstyle than usual, Pacino dresses in leather throughout most of the picture and at one point employs an eyebrow pencil before going out for the evening. (Why he would use makeup before going to a bar frequented by "butch" gay men who disdain sterotypical effeminacy is never explained.) At first, he looks realistically uncomfortable dancing with and among men in the crowded bars, but eventually he loosens up and really works himself into a sweat.

As already noted, Pacino doesn't really have that much to do in *Cruising*—the film consists mostly of wild inside glimpses of the goings-on in gay leather bars, with an occasional murder thrown in for good measure—but he is allowed two good opportunities to emote. The first has him telling his captain (Paul Sorvino) that he just can't handle the assignment; it's just too weird, and it's having a bad effect on him.

He vividly gets across Burns's fear and stress and near panic without any overacting. Later on, he gives us a bona fide Pacino blast when gay neighbor Ted's bitchy roommate, Greg, calls him "trash." Reacting negatively (to put it mildly) to Greg's insinuation that he's in love with Ted, Pacino starts hollering and trying to kick his door down. (This, of course, sets up Ted's murder. Burns—if he *is* the killer—doesn't murder Greg, but the object of his alleged affection, Ted; hence, he's "killing" his homosexual feelings.)

Is Burns Ted's killer? In Walker's novel, he was, and he was supposed to be in the movie, too. (The implication is still very much there.) Responding to gay protesters, who understandably objected to the insinuation that exposure to the gay subculture would turn one into a homicidal maniac (assuming that was ever what Friedkin intended to suggest), Friedkin made the ending more ambiguous.

Another possibility as *Ted's* killer (as opposed to the serial killer who is operating at the beginning of the film) is Patrolman DeSimone (Joe Spinell). We first see DeSimone and a partner in their police car early in the picture. When two gay guys walk by (improbably clad half in drag and half in leather!), DeSimone starts hassling them. Later on, one of the "queens" tells Sorvino that DeSimone forced him to give him a blow job.

DeSimone is later clearly seen cruising Pacino both in a leather bar and in Central Park. At the end of the picture, he is one of the officers in the apartment where Ted's bloody body has been found. Sorvino looks suspicious when DiSimone introduces himself and he recognizes the name. Has the closet-queen cop moved a step up from harassment to murder?

Ted's murder after the arrest of the main suspect in the serial killings certainly confuses the issue (not to mention the audience) but ultimately points to the true solution of the mystery. We never actually see Stuart Richards murder anyone. True, he pulls a knife during his park confrontation with Pacino, but so does Pacino. We do, however, clearly see the face of the killer in the first murder scene early in the picture— *and it isn't Stuart Richards.* To further confound us, this first killer *becomes the victim* when the killer strikes "again" in Central Park (about midway through the film). This time we don't see the killer's face, but he has the same body type as Stuart Richards. (The killer in the third murder sequence, in a porno movie theater, is hardly glimpsed at all.) All three or so killers

113

Most of the picture is over before Steve finally gets around to doing some detective work; here he questions one of the bartenders.

sing the same childish refrain—"Who's here, I'm here, you're here"—before the murders.

So what's going on here? Who the hell is the killer? The clue lies in writer-director Friedkin's having directed *The Exorcist*, with its theme of the *transference of evil*, a theme which he (mistakenly) uses once again in *Cruising*. The evil force responsible for the murders apparently moves from victim to killer to victim to killer, the killer becoming the victim and so on down the line. If this *is* what Friedkin was aiming

for, it was ill advised and poorly executed, only serving to perplex viewers and water down a gruesomely fascinating story line.

While the picture was being filmed in Greenwich Village, hundreds of gays and their supporters came out into the streets to protest, the feeling being that *Cruising* would present only the ugly, negative side of gay life and not offer any positive *human* illumination. To a large extent, this is true. Like the novel it was based on, *Cruising* presents no three-dimensional

114

characters at all, gay or straight. Pacino's part is badly underwritten, as is Sorvino's. We barely get to know Burns's pleasant gay neighbor Ted. And as Pacino's girlfriend, Nancy, Karen Allen has so little to do that her part amounts to a cameo. The screenplay never rises above its penny-dreadful origins. Had it included *real people* that we could care about, it would only have enhanced the macabre, fascinating aspects of the production. As it is, *Cruising* holds the attention, but on no deeper a level than, say, the average *Friday the 13th* installment.

Still, the picture does have several memorable sequences. The first murder is greatly enhanced by the performance of Pacino look-alike Arnaldo Santana. (In fact, the film is filled with Pacino look-alikes, creating more obfuscation.) Santana is tied up on the bed by the killer, who sadistically teases him, asking if the ropes are too tight when all along he intends to kill him. Santana evokes the terror of the victim so convincingly that the scene is very disturbing and nearly repellent. This is no "fun" cinematic murder you can distance yourself from. Santana not only resembles

Pacino encounters killer number one in Central Park.

115

Pacino, he does an excellent imitation of his acting style. Perhaps in some alternate universe Santana is the star and Pacino the supporting player.

Friedkin used openly gay extras in the gay-bar scenes, which is why they seem so spirited and realistic. And, yes, that *is* sex (real, not simulated) going on in the background, often of a particularly outré variety even by gay standards. These scenes, with a pounding rock soundtrack, are filled with energy, but they certainly scared off some of the critics. Although *Cruising* was almost universally excoriated, in some cases it wasn't clear if the reviewer objected to the films "homophobia" or its homoerotic content, indeed its essentially homophilic nature.

Unlike the source novel, the film set its story amid the sadomasochistic subculture of the gay community. (S and M, or "leather," bars, gay or straight, attract patrons who range from those merely interested in a more masculine atmosphere to those into heavy role-playing.) *Cruising* contains a disclaimer, engendered by activists' protests, stating that the picture deals with only one fragment of the gay community. Others argued that there was nothing wrong with the leather scene or with scenes of gay men enjoying themselves with abandon (in pre-AIDS days).

Before long, different factions in the community were at each other's throats. Columnist Rex Reed suggested that articles about gay murders written by the *Village Voice*'s Arthur Bell—who was a vociferous op-ponent of the movie—were far worse than anything in *Cruising,* prompting the vituperative Bell to write an article "Will the Real Rex Reed Stand Up!" which claimed that much of Reed's work was ghostwritten. Bell also got into hissy fits with Pete Hammill and others.

On the production end, James Contner's photography of smoky bars, nighttime streets, and such well-known New York City locations as Columbia University, the Central Park Ramble, the Fourteenth Street meat market, and St. James Hotel is always evocative. Jack Nitzsche's score contains hardly any real music but is filled with atmospheric electronic "sounds." The film is well cast right on down to the smaller roles, which include Ed O'Neil (of *Married With Children*) as a homicide detective who tails Pacino when Burns is wearing a wire and Powers Boothe as a salesman in a gay sex shop.

This was the second time Pacino had played a "gay/bisexual" role—sort of, leading to the usual tiresome speculation: Was *he* a closet case, a "Don Juan homosexual" romancing a series of women to cover up his true nature? What was going on in his mind while he filmed such steamy homoerotic sequences (in which he was always more of an observer than participant)?

Whatever Pacino's reasons for doing the picture, *Cruising* did nothing for his career—or anyone else's. It disappeared from theaters in a matter of days.

Pacino comes on to killer number two (or three or four or . . .) again in Central Park.

116

AUTHOR! AUTHOR!

20th Century–Fox, 1982

Producer, Irwin Winkler; director, Arthur Hiller; director of photography, Victor J. Kemper; editor, William Reynolds; music, Dave Grusin; screenplay, Israel Horovitz; production designer, Gene Rudolph. Running time: 110 min.

CAST

Al Pacino (*Ivan Trevalian*); Tuesday Weld (*Gloria*); Dyan Cannon (*Alice Detroit*); Alan King (*Kreplich*); Bob Dishy (*Finestein*); Bob Elliott (*Patrick Dicher*); Ray Goulding (*Jackie Dicher*); Eric Gurry (*Igor*); Ari Meyers (*Debbie*); Benjamin H. Carlin (*Geraldo*); B. J. Barie (*Spike*); Frederic Kimball (*Larry Kotzwinkle*); Florence Anglin (*Bag Lady*); James Tolkan (*Lieutenant Glass*); Ken Sylk (*Roger Schlesinger*).

Sitting among them, Pacino *gives* the audience a big smile in *Author! Author!*

Al Pacino couldn't have chosen a project more different from his last one, *Cruising,* than *Author! Author!*, a family comedy with him as husband and father to many children, though not always in the biological sense. Unfortunately, *Author! Author!* wasn't exactly a step upward in either screenplay or entertainment value. Perhaps in an effort to erase the stigma of *Cruising,* Pacino too readily accepted this project, written by Israel Horovitz, in whose play *The Indian Wants the Bronx* Pacino had appeared some years earlier. Pacino should have thought of a different way to repay a professional favor.

Playwright Ivan Trevalian (Pacino) has just turned forty-three. His irresponsible wife, Gloria (Tuesday Weld), goes off with another man, leaving Ivan to care for their son, Igor (Eric Gurry), as well as his many stepchildren from Gloria's previous marriages. Ivan has an affair with Alice Detroit (Dyan Cannon), the star of his new play *English With Tears,* which needs a new second act. Ivan finds it nearly impossible to work on the play; he is too busy trying to keep his

117

stepkids from being sent back to their respective fathers. In desperation he runs up to Massachusetts to get Gloria back from her lover, but discovers that he (Pacino) no longer wants her. Alice and Ivan come to an amicable separation; and Ivan revises his play. The review in the *New York Times* is favorable, Ivan gets to keep all the kids, and all is right with the world.

Frankly, Al Pacino is *miscast* as a devoted family man. Ivan Trevalian is a Jack Lemmon or Woody Allen role, and both would have been better in the part. One senses that Pacino can be very funny personally, but he hasn't that required "light touch" on camera. His Trevalian always seems as if he's on the edge of violence. Pacino can be great at broad comedy (to which *Dick Tracy* would later attest) and be awfully amusing in certain roles (*Scarecrow; Dog Day Afternoon*) that have humor written into them, but he's no Cary Grant. Besides, who really wants to see "Michael Corleone" bouncing little kids on his knee?

This is not to say that Pacino's performance is *bad;* it is just not a real Pacino role. His acting is often first-rate, such as in a scene during opening-night intermission when Ivan confesses his fears about the play, the future, that nobody else may want "Gloria's kids," to his son, Igor. "The only thing I fear," Igor tells him, "is that I inherited your nose." Pacino is very vulnerable—he seems the boy, and wise Igor, the father, soothing the "boy's" fears. It is a warmly human scene

Pacino can't help but be charmed by his sons Geraldo (Benjamin H. Carlin) and Igor.

118

Playwright Ivan Trevalian (Pacino) at home with his brood.

Ivan takes a jog through Manhattan with plucky son Igor (Eric Gurry).

in a movie that has too few of them. Young Eric Gurry, as Igor, plays up to Pacino every step of the way.

Understandably, this family comedy is short of Pacino blasts, but our hero does get across a few zingers. "I'm at the goddamn typewriter because I'm a goddamn writer!" he screams at one point. When Gloria finally comes home after a few days' disappearance, he snaps, "Where have you been? *Answer me!*" Viewers cheer when Trevalian finally tells off his wife when he tracks her down in Massachusetts. "I don't want you back. You are a cold, heartless *bitch!* Don't go in the water—give the sharks a break!"

Tuesday Weld, with whom Pacino had had an affair years earlier, is very matronly looking as the supposedly wild Gloria. Weld plays her character too straight for her ever to be likable; but she is the "villainess" of the piece. Dyan Cannon is just right as the borderline-zany Alice Detroit. When Ivan asks her at their first meeting why she's taking aspirin with her champagne, she replies, "Because champagne gives me a headache."

But the only actor who *really* registers (beside the kids) is Alan King as producer Kreplich. This is King's kind of material, and he plays it for all it is worth, making the often clichéd dialogue and stale old jokes sound fresh and inventive. King has the right "touch" throughout and is better (as is practically everyone) than the material.

In addition to Eric Gurry as Igor, child actors Benjamin H. Carlin (the insolent little Geraldo), B. J. Barie (Spike), and Ari Meyers (Debbie) are excellent. Meyers is given a particularly good scene when she sits sadly listing all her stepsiblings, stepfathers, aunts, uncles, cousins, etc. Florence Anglin and James Tolkan also score in brief bits as, respectively, a bag lady (whom Trevalian asks for an opinion of his tie) and a police officer who comes to return Debbie and her sister to their dad.

The picture sometimes summons up a spirit of fun, but such moments are few and far between. At one point, Pacino comes to the theater with a new hairdo because he got the skinny on his wife's affair from her

119

Ivan makes love to his play's lead actress (Dyan Cannon) by firelight.

120

Ivan doesn't know how his play
will be received, but at least he
looks great in a tux.

hairdresser. Trying to talk to his wife for ten minutes
at the school where she teaches, he heads off her
objections by asking, "What's the class?" "Conversation," she tells him. "Well," he says, "can't they just
chat?" When the play's director is the only one who
doesn't want to hire an actor everyone else likes, Pacino says to King: "Fire *him*."

Author! Author! is an odd mixture of inside theatrical
hipness (none of which is very compelling) and contrived sentimentality. The characters never seem like
real people, and the complications and conflicts are
as stupid and phony as all get-out. One idiotic development has Pacino taking the girls who ran away from
their father up to the roof of his apartment house in

an attempt to escape the officers sent to escort them home. In the street below more cops arrive, and a crowd gathers while Pacino yells down to the girls' father, Roger (Ken Sylk). None of this is even remotely funny.

Of course, one might ask if the shattered home lives of unwanted (by their mother) children is really a fit subject for a "comedy" to begin with. Another problem is that Ivan Trevalian is an irritating character, a suc-cessful playwright who doesn't revel in it but moans about his lot in life and takes his kids with him to show-biz hangouts like Elaine's, where he looks bored and uncomfortable. Who can feel sympathetic toward someone who can't enjoy his—how awful!—success.

Author! Author! has a Neil Simon plotline but is done mostly without wit or charm. Arthur Hiller hardly "directs" at all—the usual case with this impersonal, mediocre filmmaker. Composer Dave Grusin's pop

122

tunes on the soundtrack are pleasant but unmemorable. There are some nice shots of New York City locations, such as Sheridan Square, Waverly Place, and other Village spots, as well as Roseland and the theater district.

Author! Author! may not be Pacino's worst film, but it's the one few Pacino fans will want to see again.

Opening-night jitters shared by Alan King, Al Pacino, and Bob Dishy as, respectively, producer, writer, and director.

Ivan clowns around with his adorable youngsters.

123

SCARFACE

Universal, 1983

Executive producer, Louis A. Stroller; producer, Martin Bregman; director, Brian De Palma; director of photography, John A. Alonzo; editors, Jerry Greenberg and David Ray; screenplay, Oliver Stone; music, Giorgio Moroder; art director, Ed Richardson; visual consultant, Ferdinando Scarfiotti. Running time: 170 min.

CAST

Al Pacino (*Tony Montana*); Steven Bauer (*Manny*); Michelle Pfeiffer (*Elvira*); Mary Elizabeth Mastrantonio (*Gina*); Robert Loggia (*Frank Lopez*); Paul Shenar (*Alejandro Sosa*); Arnaldo Santana (*Ernie*); F. Murray Abraham (*Omar*); Miriam Colón (*Mama Montana*); Pepe Serna (*Angel*); Dennis Holahan (*Banker*); Harris Yulin (*Bernstein*); Richard Delmonte (*Fernando*); Richard Belzer (*MC*).

Sidney (*Dog Day Afternoon*) Lumet was the first choice to direct *Scarface*, but he wanted to make changes in the script, add a political subtext, that would make the movie less of a "cartoon" (which is ultimately what *Scarface* is). Brian De Palma, who had nearly directed Pacino in *Cruising*, was called in to helm the feature instead. Since De Palma did not work on the script—as is his usual wont—*Scarface* has few of the director's typical personal flourishes. For that sort of thing, De Palma fans would have to be satisfied with the likes of *Body Double* and *Dressed to Kill*.

Oliver Stone based his screenplay on the original film's, written by Ben Hecht in 1932. (The 1983 version of *Scarface* is dedicated to Hecht and Howard Hawks, who directed the 1932 version with Paul Muni as star.) In the original picture, Scarface was a bootlegger; Stone made him a cocaine dealer. Stone retained the subplot of the gangster's incestuous feelings for his sister but made them much more overt. He later claimed that De Palma's direction so stretched out some scenes that other scenes which helped delineate the characters had to be omitted.

Tony Montana (Pacino) is one of tens of thousands of Cuban refugees (20 percent of whom were from the criminal classes) arriving in Miami in May 1980. His first antisocial action on American soil is to carry out a hit during the turmoil of a riot at Immigration. Later, he's recruited by Frank Lopez (Robert Loggia), a drug kingpin with a haughty girlfriend, Elvira (Michelle Pfeiffer). Determined to make money and thereby have power, as Lopez does, Tony moves onward and upward in the drug trade, eventually replacing Lopez and marrying Elvira.

Tony's mother wants nothing to do with him, but

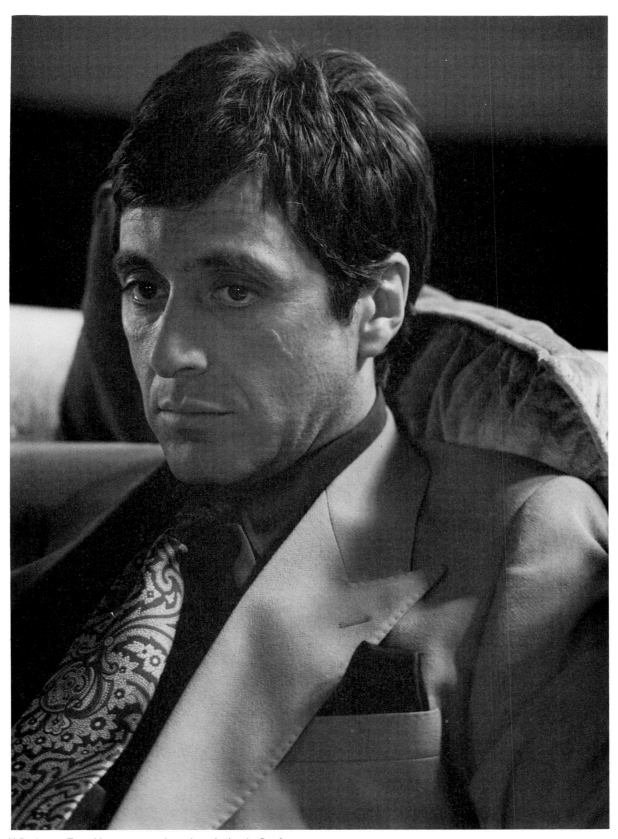

Al Pacino as Tony Montana, notorious drug dealer, in *Scarface*.

his sister Gina (Mary Elizabeth Mastrantonio), fascinated by his glamorous lifestyle, falls in love with Tony's friend and partner, Manny (Steven Bauer). But Tony has incestuous feelings for Gina and murders Manny when he finds them together, just before Gina screams at him that she and Manny had been married. Elvira walks out on Tony, Gina taunts him and shoots at him, and finally a defiant-to-the-end Montana succumbs to the bullets of a small army sent to finish him by a rival drug dealer.

With his shaggy dry haircut (as opposed to the slicked-down look of *The Godfather, Part II*) and bantamweight, cocky authority, Pacino is in full command of all he surveys in *Scarface*. He is charming, polite, proud, obscene, vulgar, and mesmeric all in a single sequence—and then some. He struts through the picture with intensity, cool aplomb, and total authority.

Scarface is many fans' favorite Pacino performance. Hard-to-please critic and film historian Lawrence J. Quirk, devotee chiefly of Hollywood's golden age, was so bowled over by Pacino in *Scarface* that he says, "Edward G. Robinson, Cagney, Paul Muni—none of them could hold a candle to Pacino when Pacino's playing a gangster. He's like a male Bette Davis on a *rampage*. Al Pacino is a *star!*"

The only negative is that Pacino's diction in this

Cuban refugee Tony Montana is determined to make it big in America—any way he has to.

Brandy, good cigars—Tony gets his first taste of "the good life."

is occasionally horrendous, and the thick accent he affects doesn't help. The Cuban accent is thicker at some times than at others, but this isn't necessarily unrealistic. What *is* unrealistic is that Tony and his buddy Manny would speak English to each other when alone. Subtitles anyone?

Montana's insolent pride, as displayed by Pacino (who clearly put some of himself in the role, remembering early insults as to his background, height, ability, etc.), is almost admirable. "Don't call me no fuckin' dishwasher," he says to one of Lopez's snotty associates. (When bitchy Elvira patronizes him at first meeting, he says with breezy rudeness, "You're good-looking, got a great face, great body, but you got a look in your eye like you haven't been fucked in years.") Soaking in a magnificent, round, golden-marble bathtub the size of an automobile, Pacino hurls scatological insults at everything and everyone. "Do you have to say 'fuck' all the time?" Elvira asks him. (The "f" word is Tony's favorite.)

Naturally, *Scarface* allows Pacino to unleash plenty of his blasts, both minor and major. He drunkenly "tells off" some ritzy restaurant patrons: "You need people like me. Somebody to point the finger at and say, 'There's the bad guy.'" Referring to some rivals in the drug trade, he screams, "Fuck the Diaz brothers! I *buried* those cock-a-roaches!" He really lets loose with a blast when he busts in on his beloved kid sister and her date, who are in a stall in the men's room, snorting coke. An animal that can barely be contained, he kicks the door, hollers, lunges at the boyfriend, even hits his sister.

Pacino has a lively supporting cast in *Scarface*. Steven Bauer as handsome buddy Manny wisely underplays, creating contrast with the almost manic Montana. Manny thinks all he has to do is stick out his tongue insinuatingly at the stuck-up rich Miami blondes and they'll fall into his arms, but it doesn't work. "You have to get the money first," says Tony. "The money and the power."

Michelle Pfeiffer is properly glacial and contemptuous ("Didja just get off a banana boat?") but not really *common* enough as the sluttish, stupid, and utterly amoral Elvira. Mary Elizabeth Mastrantonio, as Gina, has a very convincing accent but is also saddled with the biggest, bushiest "Afro" in creation. "You have some nerve!" she screams at Tony. "I'll fuck who I want to fuck!" (Fifty percent of Oliver Stone's screenplay is the "f" word, in fact.)

Mastrantonio's big scene is a very sleazy but undeniably bravura one at the end of the picture, after Tony has murdered her husband. Clad in a sexy negligee and carrying a handgun, Gina walks toward Tony in his study. "Is this what you want? Why don't you fuck me? Is this what you want, Tony?" *Bang, bang.* She keeps firing at him but fails to kill him. Mastrantonio's performance is good, and both she and Pfeiffer went on to bigger and better vehicles.

Brian De Palma (*left*) directs Al Pacino as *Scarface*.

Robert Loggia is terrific as drug lord Lopez, with his white suit and the chains around his neck. His big scene has him begging for his life after Tony learns that he ordered a hit on him in a nightclub. Tony, of course, blows him away, but he does spare Lopez's bodyguard Ernie, played by Arnaldo Santana. Santana was the Pacino look-alike who gets murdered in *Cruising*, but he doesn't look much like Pacino in *Scarface*. Harris Yulin also scores as the corrupt narcotics detec-

tive Bernstein; it's a slick, smooth, subtle performance (in a film in which subtlety is in scant supply).

One of the best performances is by Miriam Colón as Tony's mother. Her haunted expression of disillusionment over her boy, mixed emotions about seeing him, and deep reservations about his being a part of his sister's life is worth a million words. When Tony hands her a thousand dollars, this mother with no illusions instantly snaps, "Who did you kill for this, Antonio?" When her son apologizes for taking so long to get in touch, she sniffs: "No postcards in jail, huh?" Mother Montana provides some balance to the film's depiction of the Cuban-American community. "It's Cubans like you who are giving a bad name to Cubans who come here, who work hard." But the mother is more than just a positive spokesperson; Colón makes her entirely believable and human.

Scarface is quite long—nearly three hours—but is filled with memorably exciting sequences. First there's the drug deal (in the apartment) that goes sour. A woman who sits calmly on the bed watching television as the men talk actually has a shotgun hidden under her newspaper, which she employs when all hell breaks loose a moment later. Montana and an associate are dragged into the bathroom and chained to the shower rod, whereupon one character employs a chainsaw to remove the associate's limbs. (Fortunately, this all occurs mostly off camera. De Palma had to cut shots of limbs being severed to avoid an X rating.) As Pacino waits his turn, there comes an excellent crane shot that goes from the bathroom all the way down to a car on the street, where Manny, unaware of what is happening, chats with a girl, and all the way back up to the bathroom.

Eventually, Bauer comes to Pacino's rescue, resulting in an expertly edited sequence where he bursts in, machine gun blazing, the chainsaw goes flying, and Pacino pursues the fiend who made chop suey of his friend and shoots him point-blank on the street in front of dozens of horrified spectators.

The attack on Tony in the nightclub is also well handled, though it's hard to believe the would-be assassins hit him only once instead of turning him into a messy wedge of Swiss cheese. (The comic doing Ricky Ricardo imitations isn't so lucky, however.) The climactic assault on Montana's ostentatious estate by the forces of rival Alejandro Sosa (Paul Shenar) is the liveliest scene in the picture (again Pacino seems as invulnerable as Superman against so many bullets!),

Tony waits patiently to murder the drug kingpin who ordered an unsuccessful hit on him.

Now Tony sits on the king-pin's throne, the new Mr. Big Shot.

with Montana sticking a kind of mini–grenade launcher between his legs and chortling, "Say hello to my little friend."

When Tony/Pacino goes out, he goes out in style, collapsing off his balcony with his arms spread out defiantly and landing in the pool below with a mighty splash. Tony Montana has finally been brought down in a very "dramatic" larger-than-life exit. Pacino fans could ask for no more.

The "quieter" scenes in the picture (with Pacino as star, there are very few of them) sometimes work and sometimes do not. Pacino kills an assassin sent by the South American drug cartel to silence an antidrug crusader when he learns that the man also plans to blow up the victim's wife and kids. The sequence showing Tony and the hit man in their car trailing the victim and family in *their* car (with a bomb attached to the undercarriage)—Montana registering discomfort

Tony surveys the scene with buddy and partner Manny (Steven Bauer).

131

but uncertain how to proceed—is suspenseful and compelling. Tony's murder of the assassin (before he can blow up the car) angers the South Americans and leads to his undoing; ironically, it's the only decent thing he's ever done. It is because of this action that the army descends upon his estate. (Of course, Montana never considers how the woman and children would feel about their husband and father being murdered.)

On the other hand, a restaurant confrontation between Pacino and Pfeiffer is less successful. The dialogue in this sequence holds certain truths about these people, about their marriage and Tony's profession, but would these people be able to articulate these

Tony relaxes in his ostentatious bathtub as Manny expostulates.

Tony doesn't like it, but handsome Manny has eyes for sister Gina.

133

Nothing's too good for Tony, not even a tuxedo.

truths so well? Would they even *think* such thoughts, let alone verbalize them? Perhaps De Palma had good reason to cut much of Stone's screenplay. These are not exactly people who spend much time analyzing their lives and actions, after all.

This blood-drenched remake for the eighties is energetic, fun, and vivid, but—let's face it—*Scarface* is a real junk movie. If you thought the "heroes" of the *Godfather* films were bad, the main characters of *Scarface* are absolutely on the bottom of the food chain. And yes, they are romanticized a bit, even with

that "crime does not pay" finale. This is perhaps the main difference (even with all the graphic language and violence) between the 1983 *Scarface* and the 1932 original.

Writing in the September 1932 issue of *Photoplay*, editor James R. Quirk (uncle of the aforementioned Lawrence) claimed that Scarface deglamorized criminality, that the title character was not a "shrewd, exciting personality" but "a criminal moron . . . a half-mad killer, a man set apart from other men." Quirk calls Scarface "a coward . . . he dies yellow."

134

Tony lusts for his sister, Gina (Mary Elizabeth Mastrantonio), who desperately needs an appointment at the beauty parlor.

Down but not out, Tony tries to fight off his antagonists.

135

This is quite different from the way Pacino's Tony Montana goes to his death while fighting back with defiance and courage.

Note also that Montana is not brought down by police or FBI agents but by rival drug dealers. As well, *Scarface* makes the point that the U.S. government spends millions fighting the drug industry, which is in turn supported by other millions from American customers in the United States.

The over-the-top 1983 *Scarface* is a product of its time. Nowadays, there are *too many* Tony Montanas.

Tony is determined to go out in a blaze of gory glory.

REVOLUTION

Warner Brothers, Goldcrest and Viking, 1985

Executive producer, Chris Burt; producer, Irwin Winkler; director, Hugh Hudson; director of photography, Bernard Lutic; editor, Stuart Baird; screenplay, Robert Dillon; music, John Corigliano; production designer, Assheton Gorton; costume designer, John Mollo. Running time: 125 min.

CAST

Al Pacino (*Tom Dobb*); Donald Sutherland (*Sgt. Major Peasy*); Nastassja Kinski (*Daisy*); Sid Owen (*Young Ned*); Dexter Fletcher (*Older Ned*); Joan Plowright (*Mrs. McConnahy*); Dave King (*Mr. McConnahy*); Malcolm Terris (*Dr. Sloan*); Annie Lenox (*Liberty Woman*); Eric Milota (*Merle*).

Director Hugh Hudson (*Chariots of Fire; Greystoke: The Legend of Tarzan, Lord of the Apes*) had the idea of making a sort of silent-movie epic with sound when he started work on *Revolution*. The Revolutionary War itself was to be the star, with select characters moving in and out of the tapestry in much the way that they did in D. W. Griffith's silent masterpiece *Birth of a Nation*, about the Civil War. Hudson wished to eschew normal filmic storytelling and let the action speak for itself, at the expense of the narrative. Even nominal "star" Al Pacino, when he found himself getting few close-ups, wondered why Hudson was paying him so much money if he wasn't going to use him to his fullest capacity.

A force of thirty-thousand redcoats is preparing to march on New York City; to head them off, a people's army is rapidly being gathered. Tom Dobb (Al Pacino), an apolitical fur trader, is forced to give up his boat to "drive the British out of Brooklyn." While Dobb tries to redeem the temporarily worthless note he was given in exchange for the boat, his son Ned signs up as a drummer boy in the army. Dobb objects vociferously but is himself forced to join up for a payment of five shillings.

Injured after his first battle, Dobb is given food and succor by Daisy McConnahy (Nastassja Kinski), whose father is collaborating with the British for money. "It doesn't matter who deserves to win; it's who *does* win," he tells his daughter. "Now, you remember that the next time you're out there screaming liberty." Concerned primarily with his son's welfare amid the madness of war, Dobb deserts with the boy and returns to New York, where he earns both Daisy's and young Ned's enmity. When Ned is spirited off by Peasy, the head of the redcoats (Donald Sutherland), Dobb follows him and effects a rescue. Dobb ultimately be-

Pacino as Tom Dobb in *Revolution*.

Rebel forces fly the flag and plan their next maneuver.

comes an army scout at Valley Forge, where Daisy is apparently killed fleeing from Peasy. Three years later, however, she and Dobb are reunited in Yorktown. "Ain't no one ever gonna treat nobody like a dog in the dirt in this country," Dobb intones.

Not since *Cruising* had a Pacino film received such a critical drubbing as *Revolution*. First to enflame the ire of the critics was the casting of the very contemporary Pacino as a Revolutionary War hero (albeit a reluctant one). To hear them tell it, it was another case of Tony Curtis croaking, "Yondah lies da castle of my faddah" in a medieval costume epic. It seems

Young Ned (Sid Owen) and Dobb are conscripts in the Revolutionary War.

native New Yorkers were not allowed to do period pieces in which traditionally the accents (by way of Hollywood) were upper-crust and European in flavor. But the one critic who liked the picture asked: "Who knows how they talked two hundred years ago?"

True, Pacino takes some getting used to. He has a naturalistic acting style and contemporary accent that is quite different from the usual stylized approach to period dramas; sometimes he seems like an "East Side Kid" or "Bowery Boy" magically transplanted in time to the 1700s. But he is actually quite effective as Tom Dobb, skillfully getting across the character of a man who just wants to protect his son, stay out of trouble, and get on with his interrupted life more than anything. (Pacino's one concession to the period is the small pigtail he wears.)

Pacino is given several powerful scenes, such as when he finds out that his son has been compelled to sign up with the army and is himself forced into conscription by rebels who won't take no for an answer. His rage and frustration at the unfairness of it is almost palpable. He admirably evinces Dobb's fear and determination to stay alive during a grotesque "fox hunt" in which British officers set dogs on Pacino, a colleague, and an effigy of George Washington they must drag along with them. Cornered by a sneering redcoat, Pacino braces himself for the killing stroke, but the officer sticks his sword in the effigy instead.

By far Pacino's greatest scene is when some friendly Indians tend to the badly injured feet and legs of young Ned after Dobb has rescued the boy from the British. Ned is in great pain and near death; as the Indians work on his lower extremities, Dobb holds Ned and comforts him, exhibiting such great intensity, paternal passion, and "hopeful despair" as he begs his son not to die that he seems to be *living* it instead of just acting. It is moments like this that show why Pacino can almost always triumph over "miscasting" with shear acting virtuosity.

Because it is the emotionalism and not the dialogue that carries this scene, its efficacy is not blunted by Pacino's unfortunate mumbling throughout. Pacino is often mush-mouthed in *Revolution,* which was certainly a factor in the bad notices he received. Not only a Bronx accent, the critics thought, but such impenetrable diction! His goodbye speech to his son at the end of the picture is nearly unintelligible. Better, some thought, if Hudson *had* done a "silent movie" with subtitles. Undoubtedly, Hudson was carried away

The rebels prepare for battle.

by Pacino's powerhouse emoting, but why didn't he just say: "Al, love, maybe the audience would kind of like to know what you're *saying.*" At least Pacino had more of an excuse in *Scarface,* what with his Cuban accent.

A minor Pacino blast occurs when Dobb finds out that the U.S. government can't make good on its promise to reimburse veterans with parcels of land. "What happened to the 150 acres I was promised?" he hollers, looking as if he's about to grab somebody and start chewing on them any second.

Compared to poor Donald Sutherland, as Sgt. Major Peasy, Pacino seems like Oscar material. Sutherland *looks* the part, all right, radiating evil authority, but his acting and speech (British accent notwithstanding) leave something to be desired. Somebody should have told him he was not in a Victor Herbert operetta. Warner Brothers wanted the loathsome Peasy to die so that the audience could experience some catharsis, but Hudson saw him as the spirit of England and just lets him wander off at the end after a pallid "confrontation" with Pacino. The "Snidely Whiplash" nature of the British soldiers isn't helped by the fact that they are generally depicted as overaged bullies and border-line pedophiles.

Nastassja Kinski is fine as Daisy McConnahy, who is as patriotic as her father is not. The spirited Daisy wants nothing to do with the British. When her father and mother entertain them in their home, Daisy stabs one would-be lothario with an American flag pin. His wig falls off as he jumps up and screams, "Yankee bitch!" To Daisy's parents he yells, "Your daughters are *whores*!" Kinski also figures in a moving, evocative sequence when she allows a doctor operating on a screaming, frightened boy to use her shawl as a tourniquet. Daisy was supposed to die—and stay dead—in the film, but Warner Brothers insisted she be brought back and reunited with Pacino in an epilogue. Hudson won his point with Peasy/Sutherland but lost with Daisy/Kinski.

The "relationship" between Daisy and Tom Dobb seems to come out of nowhere, however. Pacino spends more time hugging and kissing his son than he does Nastassja, and she evokes little emotion in him. Hudson muffs a "romantic" scene in which Pacino runs after Kinski's wagon as she rides away, declaring his love as she does the same—all in long shot. (The bit with the redcoats chasing after the wagon and "killing" Daisy immediately afterward is exciting,

however.) Dobb's true love is for his son, expertly played by Sid Owen as a young boy and Dexter Fletcher as a teenager.

The repulsive Annie Lenox of the rock group Eurythmics has a mercifully brief scene (and is almost unrecognizable) as a screeching lady rebel who helps commandeer Pacino's boat.

146

The one thing in which *Revolution* excels is in its delineation of *battle;* the redcoats lining up and literally marching off to war, the initially overwhelmed rebel forces running off in panic. The battle scenes are extremely well staged and realistic: These soldiers aren't always supremely cool and confident, they don't always know what they're doing, and there's often a natural *sloppiness* to their actions. Indeed, all the extras milling about messily (which initially seems comical) manage to approximate the confusion of the period. *Revolution* vividly gets across the ugliness, tedium, grimness, boredom, and loneliness of war. Its matter-of-fact approach to sudden death is all the more chilling and poignant.

Tom substitutes for the fox in a "foxhunt" organized by British officers with a sick sense of humor.

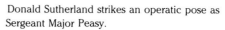
Donald Sutherland strikes an operatic pose as Sergeant Major Peasy.

Tom Dobb just wants to be left alone to ply his trade and wants no part of politics.

New Yorkers were a rowdy bunch even back then.

Dobb is taken captive
temporarily.

Daisy (Nastassja Kinski), a
loyal American, is still wor-
ried over her man, Tom.

As well, its production designer, Assheton Gorton, costume designer, John Mollo, and others expertly re-create the period with terrific settings, elaborate outfits, and thousands of teeming extras going in every which direction but up. Bernard Lutic's photography offers some superb shots of a pristine countryside and cluttered cityscape, but the wavering, handheld-camera cinéma vérité approach isn't always efficacious. John Corigliano's musical score is nice and atmospheric.

The tragedy with the ambitious *Revolution* is that it starts off so well and *collapses* so completely in the second half. The many missteps indicate a director who is overwhelmed and not in full command of his production. For every scene that works, there are two that are completely devoid of cinematic authority. Robert Dillon's screenplay sets up some interesting and unpredictable conflicts, but they are all muted by the meandering direction. Directed by William Wyler or even "One Take" Woody Van Dyke in Hollywood's golden age, *Revolution* might have emerged as a classic. Hugh Hudson knew what he wanted, but this time the talented director couldn't quite get his vision on the screen. Which is not something to bitchily chortle over, as many reviewers did; it is something to *mourn*. All that hard work, fine acting by Pacino, great period detail—what a picture *Revolution* could have been!

It would be four years before Al Pacino would make another movie.

SEA OF LOVE

Universal, 1989

Producers, Martin Bregman and Louis A. Stroller; director, Harold Becker; director of photography, Ronnie Taylor; editor, David Bretherton; screenplay, Richard Price; music, Trevor Jones; associate producer, Michael Scott Bregman; production designer, John Jay Moore; costume designer, Betsy Cox. Running time: 112 min.

CAST

Al Pacino (*Frank Keller*); Ellen Barkin (*Helen*); John Goodman (*Sherman*); William Hickey (*Frank Sr.*); Michael Rooker (*Terry*); Christine Estabrook (*Gina Gallagher*); Richard Jenkins (*Greber*); Michael Fischetti (*Doorman*); Michael O'Neill (*Raymond Brown*); Patricia Barry (*Older Woman*).

Al Pacino as Detective Frank Keller in *Sea of Love.*

After the debacle of *Revolution* four years earlier, *Sea of Love* was considered by many to be Pacino's "comeback" film.

The movie begins with the murder of a nude, panicked man who is shot in his bed as the record "Sea of Love" plays on the phonograph. Called in to investigate is Detective Frank Keller (Pacino), who is embittered because his ex-wife married another cop, with whom he often crosses paths. Keller teams up with another detective, Sherman (John Goodman), who has had a similar murder in his own jurisdiction. The two cook up a scheme to catch the killer by placing a personal ad in a singles' publication.

151

Keller is having one of those days.

One clear suspect emerges: Helen (Ellen Barkin). As Keller finds himself sexually and romantically drawn to the woman, things keep happening which make him more and more suspicious of her, especially the fact that she dated all (by now) three murdered men. Helen is furious to find out that he's a cop and breaks up with him. The killer is eventually unveiled: Helen's jealous ex-husband. Keller patches things up with Helen.

Pacino is a bit (deliberately) schlumpy in *Sea of Love*, but he looks good and acts well. He gets into some hot, animalistic love scenes with Barkin—rough, slightly kinky, up against the walls, and so on—which reveal that Pacino has kept himself in good shape. It's quite possible that Pacino did this picture when he was pushing fifty just to show he could keep up his vital, virile image with the best of them. That plus the fact that it seemed like a sure crowd pleaser after the more "acquired taste" of *Revolution*.

Richard Price's screenplay is no world-beater by any objective standards, but it does give Pacino a chance to quietly (for a change) practice his craft. He's like a little lost puppy begging Barkin not to be mad at him and quite funny when he has dinner with her at a fancy restaurant where there are no waiters, no menu, but an annoying violinist. "Can you get the waiter?" he asks him. He's convincingly scared when he's being beaten by the murderous ex-husband (a very enthusiastic Michael Rooker) at the climax. He exudes that special charisma of his when he drunkenly goads Goodman to "take it off" as the latter dances at a police reception. And there's even a milder form of the Pacino blast when he gets in a fight with his ex-wife's husband immediately after the reception. The world-weary, lonely, regretful, semi-alcoholic cop is a tired old stereotype, but Pacino does his best to make Frank Keller seem like a real human being.

Detective Sherman (John Goodman) teams up with Keller to catch a killer.

Helen (Ellen Barkin) may be the killer Frank is looking for.

154

Tormented by his suspicions, Keller tries to quell his doubts.

Ellen Barkin, with her odd, crooked smile, is like the proverbial martini. In her first appearance she looks like a hooker, and the picture makes her little more than a sex object—albeit an aggressive one—for most of its running time. Since she is supposed to be a woman of mystery—did she kill those men or didn't she?—the movie can't reveal too much of her. Getting into the spirit of things, Barkin felt the film revealed too much, such as Helen's apartment, child, and mother. As it is, Helen is half real, half femme-fatale icon. Barkin plays her as well as anyone could.

John Goodman is, as usual, ingratiating, if only on the surface. William Hickey is as reliable—and as creepy—as ever as Keller's father. Michael Rooker radiates menace as Helen's ex-husband, Terry. Michael O'Neill has a nice bit as Raymond (the family man addicted to singles' ads who becomes the killer's third victim), as does Patricia Barry as the "older woman" who answers Keller's personal ad. Actually, Barry doesn't look much older than Pacino. All the smaller parts are well cast, in fact.

The picture has a few highlights, such as an early scene when Pacino welcomes a group of men into a gymnasium where they think they are going to meet the New York Yankees. "I know who you are!" one fellow says to Pacino. "Look," he tells his pals, "it's Phil Rizzuto!" But the "meet the Yankees" business is just a ploy, and the invitations are phony. The men

155

have actually been rounded up because there are outstanding warrants out on all of them. A closet bleeding heart, Keller lets one guy go who is wanted on two counts of grand theft auto because his little son is with him. (What a role model!)

The picture works up some mild suspense during Pacino and Barkin's first bedroom scene. When Helen leaves the room, Keller is sure she's going to get her gun and make him victim number four. He panics, but finds only a starter pistol in her purse. The climax, with Pacino battling the real killer, has some well-orchestrated fisticuffs, involves guns and barbells, and is fairly exciting, thanks to some good stunt work.

Although *Sea of Love* has a light touch, it doesn't quite come off as a comedy-thriller, and some "humorous" moments—such as Keller discussing why his wife left him for her new husband while leaning over the first corpse—are ill advised. Worse yet are the many moments of illogic. First, Barkin bluntly tells Keller that he's not her type, rudely walking out on him, but the next time she sees him, at a fruit stand, she picks him up! This creates suspense but makes little sense. Did the daylight turn him into "her type?" Keller makes dates with several of the women who answered his ad, at the same bar, *on the same night*. While this facilitates Goodman's retrieving their fingerprints (he's disguised as a waiter), it seems incredible that all of the women would dutifully walk off at the appropriate time so that Keller would be free to meet the next on his list. (If each date occurs on a different night, the editing certainly doesn't make that clear.)

Price's screenplay is virtually mindless, without having the clever denouement or fascinating elements that might compensate. The ending, the solution to

Detective Keller shows he can still charm with the best of them.

Sherman and Keller take turns playing singles'-ad dates and the waiter who picks up the glass with the ladies' fingerprints on it.

156

Sherman and Keller confer on the case.

Detective Keller has some words with his fellow cops.

the murders, is flat and no surprise. Goodman and Pacino laugh at one of the victims' poems in a personal-ad magazine, but the film never examines their jealousy of these cocksmen or says anything fresh or novel about the situation. What's more, it completely lacks the visceral power of *Fatal Attraction*, its obvious model.

At least Price drops in some good dialogue now and then. When Keller gets a punk would-be customer to leave the shoe store where Helen works and she

Killer she may be, but Frank still wants her—boy, does he want her!

learns that Keller is a police officer, he says: "You let creeps like that in here, but you're upset because I'm a cop? People find out I'm a cop—suddenly I'm a nonperson." After Keller points out different apartments in which murders have been committed in a building across the street as he and Helen take a walk, she looks at him and says, "This is one big city of the dead for you, isn't it?" There's some saucy dialogue from the women who answer Pacino's ad but don't believe his made-up stories. "If you're a printer," one says, "I've got a dick." "You probably do," Pacino mutters as she storms off.

The fatal ingredient in *Sea of Love* is Harold Becker's direction, which betrays absolutely no style or pacing whatsoever. Alfred Hitchcock probably would have rejected this script, but if he hadn't he would have made a picture that moved and had suspense. Instead of Bernard Herrmann on the score, we get Trevor Jones, whose music is forgettable. "Sea of Love," performed by Phil Phillips and the Twilights, is a catchy tune from the fifties at least, but it won't make people rush out to buy the soundtrack.

None of this mattered to the critics and fans, who made *Sea of Love* a hit. Pacino got some of the best reviews of his life, and his career and popularity were back on track. But one suspects that years from now *Sea of Love* will not be one of the pictures he is best remembered for.

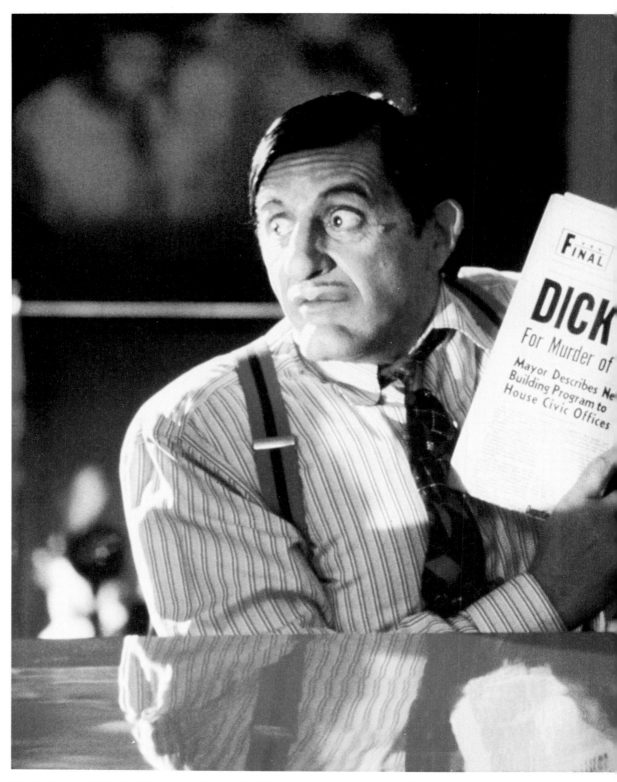

Big Boy Caprice (Al Pacino) is overjoyed to learn that his nemesis has been arrested for murder.

DICK TRACY

Touchstone, in association with Silver Screen Partners IV, 1990

Executive producers, Barrie M. Osborne, Art Linson, and Floyd Mutrux; producer, Warren Beatty; director, Beatty; director of photography, Vittorio Storaro; editor, Richard Marks; music, Danny Elfman; original songs, Stephen Sondheim; screenplay, Jim Cash and Jack Epps Jr., based on characters created by Chester Gould; production designer, Richard Sylbert; art director, Harold Michelson; set decorator, Rick Simpson; costume designer, Milena Canonero. Running time: 105 min.

CAST

Al Pacino (*Big Boy Caprice*); Warren Beatty (*Dick Tracy*); Glenne Headly (*Tess Trueheart*); Charlie Korsmo (*Kid*); Madonna (*Breathless Mahoney*); Paul Sorvino (*Lips Manlis*); Charles Durning (*Chief Brandon*); William Forsythe (*Flattop*); Dustin Hoffman (*Mumbles*); Ed O'Ross (*Itchy*); R. G. Armstrong (*Pruneface*); Dick Van Dyke (*D.A. Fletcher*); Michael J. Pollard (*Bug Bailey*); James Caan (*Spaldoni*); Mandy Patinkin (*88 Keys*); Estelle Parsons (*Mrs. Trueheart*).

Warren Beatty's production of *Dick Tracy* is due for a reevaluation. *Dick Tracy* got mixed reviews upon its release because too many critics reacted to what it wasn't instead of to what is was. Audiences were expecting a rollicking roller-coaster ride à la *Indiana Jones and the Temple of Doom* or *Batman*; they wanted their comic-book movies to be one cliffhanger after another. Because the first episode of the 1938 serial *Dick Tracy* had more thrills than the entire Beatty movie, many deemed his *Dick Tracy* a failure. Once you accept that *Dick Tracy* is an adventure movie but not a rat-a-tat-tat action flick, its pleasures are more readily apparent.

Al Pacino was chosen for the pivotal role of Tracy's prime antagonist, Big Boy Caprice. Caprice rubs out his rival Lips Manlis (Paul Sorvino) and takes over both his territory and his girl, the singer "Breathless" Mahoney (Madonna). Dick Tracy (Warren Beatty) de-clares war on the Mob, to which Caprice reacts by trying to kill him. Tracy's life is saved by a mysterious figure known only as "the Blank." The Blank kidnaps Tracy's girlfriend, Tess (Glenne Headly), and frames Tracy for the murder of the district attorney (Dick Van Dyke). Tracy rescues Tess and unmasks the Blank as voluptuous Breathless, who was playing both sides against each other in an effort to take over the city for herself. Caprice's reign of criminality is brought to a halt.

Playing a miserable warthog of a man, Pacino was certainly outfitted for the occasion. A body suit gives him a massive chest and upper body and a tremen-dous ass. Along with plastered-down hair complete with Hitlerian bangs, he has thick, ugly lips, a pencil

Warren Beatty may have been the star—and the hero—but he played second fiddle to Pacino's Big Boy.

Dick Tracy arrives at head-quarters burning for action.

mustache, an oversized honker, and an expanded, witchlike chin with a cleft. He walks hunched over all the time like a miniature Quasimodo. He ain't pretty, but his acting is superb. Pacino obviously had a ball playing Big Boy, and his performance garnered him an Oscar nomination for Best Supporting Actor.

Played by Pacino, Big Boy Caprice is almost lovable in his own rodentlike way. Pacino does a terrific, energetic parody of himself. Whether he is rubbing his hands together like a little kid and practically cackling after planting a fake message on a tape or urging Madonna to give "more, more, *more*" to her song number (appropriately entitled "More"), he proves that he's very adept at *broad*, high-impact comedy. Larger than life in *Dick Tracy*, Pacino is in a Rossini mode as opposed to the Verdi mode of *The Godfather* or *Scarface*.

But Pacino knows when to underplay. After rival Spaldoni's (James Caan) car is blown up after their meeting, Pacino quietly says, "Very upsetting," and gently pats the table. (It's an inspired touch and great fun to have "Michael Corleone" and "Sonny Corleone" facing each other down from opposite ends of the table.) Pacino also gets off some blasts as Big Boy: "There is one Napoleon!" he shouts. "One *me!*" and, "I want . . . Dick Tracy . . . *dead!*" Pacino is absolutely

hilarious as he and Tess Trueheart ride on their stomachs in a getaway underground railway car and *he never stops talking* the whole time!

Pacino's is the showiest performance, no doubt, but he is surrounded by a generally talented supporting cast. The nominal star, Warren Beatty, actually isn't bad as Dick Tracy, even if he doesn't seem as perfect for the role as his predecessor, Ralph Byrd, was. (Byrd starred as Tracy in several serials, feature films, and even a television series.) Glenne Headly is perfect—sweet, but a little saucy, too—as Tess Trueheart, who temporarily goes home to mother when Tracy fails to propose and get a desk job. Little Charlie Korsmo is excellent as Kid, the young boy who comes into their lives, saves Tracy's life, and chooses "Dick Tracy Jr." as his official moniker. Dick Van Dyke scores in an unusual role for him, as the corrupt district attorney. Beatty even gave small parts to his old *Bonnie and Clyde* costars Michael J. Pollard (a 1930s version of a wiretapper) and Estelle Parsons (Tess's mom); both deliver. "It takes a lot of understanding to love a man like that," Parsons counsels her daughter.

After Beatty and Pacino, the actor who got the most press was Madonna. Madonna is able to put over Stephen Sondheim's catchy songs (without having a particularly good voice), but as an actress she radiates more style than substance. She comes *this close* to being effective, but doesn't quite cut it. To be fair, she has a credible scene at the docks with Tracy. "Tell me you want me!" she says to him, hinting at the vulnerability and pathos beneath the surface sexiness. Beatty might have gotten even more of an *on-screen* performance out of Madonna if he hadn't been so busy romancing her at the time. "No grief for Lips?" he asks Breathless after the murder of her former boyfriend. "I'm wearing black underwear," she replies. Madonna is in her Marilyn Monroe mode throughout the movie.

Big Boy tells the members of the underworld just what they can expect now that he's taken over.

Big Boy has a chat with one of his equally repulsive confederates.

Big Boy (*background*) supervises as his men prepare a death trap for Tracy (*foreground, in chair*).

Breathless Mahoney, (Madonna) wants "more, more, *more*" in her song number.

Big Boy lays down the law to Tracy now that he's got the lawman in his clutches.

Breathless and 88 Keys (Mandy Patinkin) do a little crooning but no spooning.

Tracy confers with Kid (Charlie Korsmo) in the art deco city.

As previously stated, *Dick Tracy* lacks any really magnificent action set pieces à la the James Bond or Indiana Jones series, but it is not without its highlights just the same. One near nail-biter has Tracy tied to a chair in a basement next to a boiler that is about to explode; Kid comes to the rescue just in time. A shootout between the cops and a bunch of crooks firing from their cars with tommy guns is exciting. The business with a kidnapped Tess tied to a drawbridge's turntable and nearly crushed isn't milked for enough suspense, but it is still tense and compelling. The picture has a sense of fun, too: Tracy is called from watching a musical show to investigate the murder of Lips Manlis and others; when he returns to the theater, they're still doing the *same number*.

A stunning visual feast, *Dick Tracy* is a study in charm and whimsy and cinematic artistry. Beatty's direction is assured and confident, and editor Richard Marks gives the picture fluidity and pacing. Harold Michelson's sets and Richard Sylbert's production design are outstanding, as are the special effects and matte paintings employed to bring the wonderfully colorful (in every sense of the word) proceedings to life. Kudos also to Danny Elfman's score, Stephen Sondheim's nifty songs, and Vittorio Storaro's cinematography, which throws a glossy, striking sheen over everything.

Those who dismissed *Dick Tracy* when it was first released may find it genuinely delightful on second viewing. One thing that can't be dismissed: Pacino *is* a delight as Big Boy Caprice. He practically walks away with the picture, no mean feat indeed.

Madonna sits on Pacino's lap, but she saved her kisses for Beatty—and considering Pacino's makeup job, who could blame her?

170

THE GODFATHER, PART III

Paramount, 1990

Executive producers, Fred Fuchs and Nicholas Gage; producer, Francis Ford Coppola; director, Coppola; director of photography, Gordon Willis; editors, Barry Malkin, Lisa Fruchtman, and Walter Murch; screenplay, Mario Puzo and Coppola; music, Carmine Coppola; additional music, Nino Rota; associate producer, Marina Gefter; coproducers, Fred Roos, Gray Frederickson, and Charles Mulvehill; production designer, Dean Tavoularis; costume designer, Milena Canonero. Running time: 170 min.

CAST

Al Pacino (*Michael Corleone*); Andy García (*Vincent Mancini*); Eli Wallach (*Don Altobello*); Talia Shire (*Connie*); Sofia Coppola (*Mary*); Franc D'Ambrosio (*Anthony*); Diane Keaton (*Kay*); George Hamilton (*Harrison*); Bridget Fonda (*Grace*); John Savage (*Andrew Hogan*); Donal Donnelly (*Archbishop*); Raf Vallone (*Cardinal Lamberto*); Mario Donatone (*Mosca*); Joe Mantegna (*Joey Zasa*); Al Martino (*Johnny Fontaine*); Helmut Berger (*Frederick Kelmszig*).

Sixteen years had passed since *The Godfather, Part II*; it was time for the next—and, thus far, final—chapter in the saga of the Corleone family.

Michael Corleone's bodyguard has a message for him.

The story begins in New York City in 1979. Michael Corleone (Al Pacino) is receiving an award for his charitable work through the Corleone Foundation, which helps the impoverished and is dedicated to the rebirth of Sicily. Kay (Diane Keaton) has divorced Michael and remarried. Daughter Mary (Sofia Coppola) is chairman of the Corleone Foundation, while son Anthony (Franc D'Ambrosio) is about to make his debut as an opera singer. Sonny's illegitimate son, Vincent Mancini (Andy García), Michael's nephew, makes it known that he wants to advance in the family. He and cousin Mary begin an affair.

Michael agrees to cover losses in the Vatican bank

in return for control of Immobiliare, the Vatican corporation. His former partners want in on the deal to "purify their money," but Michael is after total legitimacy and must turn them down. He also meets resistance from the other board members of Immobiliare. After suffering a diabetic stroke, Michael tells Vincent that he'll make him head of the family but he must give up Mary. During Anthony's debut in *Cavalleria Rusticana* in Palermo, the Corleones strike to take care of their assorted enemies and attempt to save the life of Pope John Paul I, who has ratified the Immobiliare deal but is promptly murdered by opposing Vatican factions. On the steps of the opera house Michael and his daughter are both shot by assassins.

Pacino inexplicably wanted to wear his hair down to his shoulders in *Godfather III*, but director Francis Ford Coppola wisely told him *no*. Instead, he wears a more appropriate gray brush cut. His voice is very

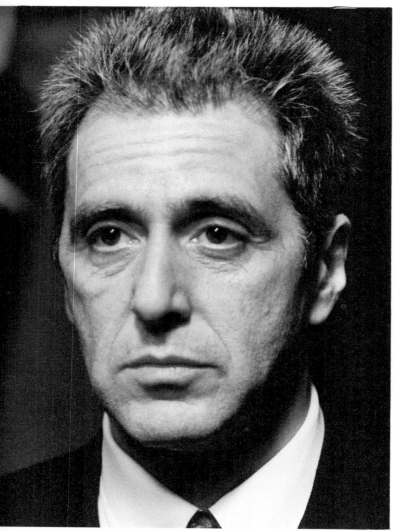

Pacino demonstrates the brush cut Coppola persuaded him to wear as Michael Corleone instead of inappropriately long tresses; perhaps the director made his star an offer he couldn't refuse.

raspy, and he seems more "common" than he was in the first two films. But he absolutely *dominates* the picture, even over such competition as the younger, energetic Andy García, as his nephew.

Pacino plays with his usual assurance and charisma and has several especially fine scenes, such as when he gives his confession to Cardinal Lamberto (Raf Vallone), who later becomes Pope John Paul I. Collapsing into tears, he says, "I murdered my mother's son, my father's son." He is also excellent reacting to Mary's death on the steps on the opera house, emitting a potent outcry of remorse and anguish. One of the few Pacino blasts in the picture occurs when Michael learns that his nephew "whacked" someone without his permission: *"It was not what I wanted!"* he screams.

Of the supporting cast, Andy Garcia, with slicked-back hair and intense expression, makes the strongest impression as the bastard nephew Vincent. While he represents the younger generation, he's an old-fashioned mafioso at heart. Michael orders Vincent to make peace with Joey Zasa (Joe Mantegna), who now owns what used to be the Corleone family business. But as Vincent grudgingly hugs his nemesis Joey, he gives the latter a bloody bite on the ear. This culminates in Vincent disguising himself as a cop on horseback and carrying through on his threat to whack Zasa by shooting him during a violent blowout in Little Italy. Later, as Vincent watches his cousin perform in *Cavalleria Rusticana,* there's an amusing cut to his laughing in appreciation after he sees Anthony's "Turridu" biting the ear of "Alfio," the man who married his lover while Turridu was in the army (and with whose wife Turridu is now sleeping).

Diane Keaton's "Kay" is the voice of common decency in the *Godfather* movies, especially in this installment. Keaton is quite effective in her confrontation with ex-husband Michael at the reception that takes place after he receives his award and is also good later in the picture when she and Michael have a few quiet moments in Sicily before their son's operatic debut. Kay and Michael are fond of each other but no longer in love—but there's still a lingering feeling and a bond. This was exactly the situation in real life. Keaton and Pacino, who had been involved with each other at different times over the years, broke up, got back together, and finally broke up for good during the shooting of *The Godfather, Part III.*

The most controversial casting was of director Coppola's daughter Sofia as Mary Corleone. Julia Roberts

Director Francis Ford Coppola (*on left*) gives some pointers to star Pacino on the set of *Godfather, Part III*.

173

Michael greets some guests who have arrived to honor him.

Michael's bastard nephew Vincent (Andy García, *right*) hangs his head while Michael wonders what to do with him.

Andy García radiates sleek, disarming menace and swagger as Vincent Mancini, Sonny's illegitimate son.

had been first choice for the part, but there were scheduling conflicts. Winona Ryder was subsequently signed, but she had to bow out due to illness from an overcrowded schedule. Finally, Coppola chose his daughter Sofia, to the amazement of Hollywood insiders, who thought he was crazy to give such an important part to an amateur. Sofia received scathing reviews, but she is actually more than adequate in the part. Just like the character she portrays, Sofia is equal parts innocence and sensuality, a full-lipped beauty with strong carnal appeal. While you wouldn't want to cast her as Blanche Du Bois in a revival of *A Streetcar Named Desire,* she's perfect as Mary Corleone.

Robert Duvall wanted too much money, so his "Tom Hagen" character was written out. Instead, there were small roles for John Savage as Hagen's son Andrew, a priest, and George Hamilton, as a new Corleone family adviser, Harrison. Eli Wallach is charming malevolence personified as the traitorous Don Altobello. Bridget Fonda appears very briefly as a reporter who sleeps with Vincent and is okay in the part. Joe Mantegna certainly makes his mark as the slimy Joey Zasa in an energetic, on-target performance. Resurfacing in a bit part as Swiss banker Frederick Kelmszig is Helmut Berger of *The Damned.* Franc D'Ambrosio hasn't much to do as Anthony Corleone, but he reveals a nice enough voice as Turridu, if not quite on the Pavarotti level. And Talia Shire emerges as a tougher, more active Connie in her ruthless portrayal of Michael's sister.

Michael is a little nervous: Vincent is getting a little too close to Michael's daughter, Mary (Sofia Coppola).

175

Vincent can't resist Mary's allure of sensuality and innocence in search of besmirchment.

The aforementioned shootouts in Little Italy and on the operahouse steps are highlights of *The Godfather, Part III* to be sure, but the most exciting scene, bar none, takes place in Atlantic City, where Michael has gathered bigwigs from all the families. Just as this gangland convention is breaking up, a sort of hurricane wind whips through the meeting hall, and an inexplicable racket fills the air. The next moment, the fleeing hoods are spattered with bullets as helicopters with machine guns fly past and over the balconies, spurting death and mayhem. Michael, of course, survives to put paid to the man who has dared to try to wipe out all competition in one fell swoop.

The ending of *The Godfather, Part III* is a reprise of the climaxes of *The Godfather* and *The Godfather, Part II*, with the Corleone family "taking care" of all their enemies in one evening. Targets include a hit man, Mosca (Mario Donatone), who tried to murder Michael in Sicily, and Don Altobello, who was behind the superhit in New Jersey. (Connie feeds the unsuspecting don some poisoned pastries.) As they watch Anthony in the opera, the Corleones are unaware that assassins are taking out their bodyguards, strangling and shooting them in draperied alcoves and deserted boxes, thereby setting up the hit on Michael on the opera steps afterward.

This opera sequence is one of the best scenes in the film, but it is not comparable to its obvious model:

Director Francis Ford Coppola (*left, in beard and glasses*) gives last-minute instructions to Joe Mantegna (*in black suit, left*) and Al Pacino. Eli Wallach (*seated*) and Andy García (*standing*) are on the right.

176

Michael's about to make Vincent an offer he can't refuse: His nephew can take over as head of the family but only if he gives up Mary for good.

the Albert Hall assassination attempt in Hitchcock's remake of his own *The Man Who Knew Too Much* (1956). Coppola's opera scene, like the picture in general, needs tightening and pacing to really make it *sing*.

Speaking of singing, a word is in order on *Cavalleria Rusticana*, the opera chosen for the background of this sequence. Composer Pietro Mascagni's 1890 masterpiece takes place in Sicily (birthplace of the Mafia) and deals with betrayal and revenge (and, most especially, unrequited love). But that's where its resemblance to the film ends. *The Godfather, Part III*, like its two predecessors, is essentially just a glossy, generally well made potboiler and nothing more. *Cavalleria*

The Corleone family and advisers attend a performance of Pietro Mascagni's masterpiece *Cavalleria Rusticana.*

The Godfather, his ex-wife, and family lawyer
(George Hamilton, *center*) attend the opera.

Francis Ford Coppola mulls over a shot from behind
the camera.

Rusticana is an immortal work of genius, depth, passion, and *sensitivity,* a brilliant examination of pathetic lives. Franco Zeffirelli's film version with Placido Domingo makes the admittedly entertaining *Godfather, Part III* seem like junk in comparison.

Al Pacino is himself an opera buff, which may be why Coppola built the opera sequence into the picture in the first place. A funny sequence in *The Godfather, Part III* has Michael Corleone proudly announcing to friends that his son will make his debut in *Cavalleeria Rusticana.* "Uh, that's *Cavallereeeah Rusticana,* Dad," corrects Anthony. Presumably, Pacino would never commit such a pronunciational faux pas. Coppola's faux pas is to present the great opera *out of sequence* in *The Godfather, Part III.*

Although Carmine Copolla and Nino Rota are credited as composers for *The Godfather, Part III,* all of the great music heard in the last twenty or so minutes is from Mascagni's opera.

Does *The Godfather, Part III* glorify the Mafia? In this picture it's the Corleone family against the rest of the Mob—making them "heroes." They even try to save the life of the pope! Their actions are continually justified, and time and again we're supposed to believe that members of the Mafia are just like everyone else. The picture makes comparisons to politics and crime that are a bit self-serving. One thing the movie doesn't gloss over is the fist-in-glove relationship between the Mafia and the Catholic Church. Cardinal Lamberto doesn't even look striken as Michael confesses his many disturbing sins (not wanting to "bite the hand that feeds him," one supposes).

But the main problem with *The Godfather, Part III* is its length and deliberate pacing. The picture would be more effective tightened and trimmed of at least a half hour's running time.

Most critics and audiences were pleased with *The Godfather, Part III* nonetheless. It received seven Academy Award nominations (including Best Picture and Best Director), but Al Pacino wasn't included. British film critic Alexander Walker risked (and some say damaged) his reputation by declaring *The Godfather, Part III* a "masterpiece."

Hardly. It was just good dirty fun.

FRANKIE AND JOHNNY

Paramount, 1991

Executive producers, Alexandra Rose and Charles Mulvehill; producer, Garry Marshall; director, Marshall; director of photography, Dante Spinotti; screenplay, Terence McNally; based on McNally's stage play *Frankie and Johnny in the Clair de Lune;* editors, Battle Davis and Jacqueline Cambas; coproducer, Nick Abdo; music, Marvin Hamlisch; production designer, Albert Brenner; costume designer, Rosanna Norton. Running time: 118 min.

CAST

Al Pacino (*Johnny*); Michelle Pfeiffer (*Frankie*); Hector Elizondo (*Nick*); Nathan Lane (*Tim*); Kate Nelligan (*Cora*); Jane Morris (*Nedda*); Fernando Lopez (*Jorge*); Glen Plummer (*Peter*); Sean O'Bryan (*Bobby*); Tim Hopper (*Lester*).

"New York City can be a dangerous, hostile place," the warden says to Johnny (Al Pacino) as the latter leaves jail after serving his sentence. "It'll be a nice change," Johnny says.

And indeed, the New York City of *Frankie and Johnny*—one of Pacino's nicest pictures—is not the New York of *The Panic in Needle Park*, with its drug addicts; *The Godfather* and sequels, with their elegant hoodlums; *Serpico,* with its corrupt police officers; or *Cruising* and *Sea of Love,* with their brutal serial murderers. Not since *Author! Author!* in 1982 had Pacino done a warm, comic film. Even better, *Frankie and Johnny*—unlike *Author! Author!*—was a *good* picture.

Johnny has spent one and a half years in jail for forging a check. He goes to work as a cook at the Apollo Restaurant at Ninth Avenue and Twenty-third Street and is almost immediately smitten with a pretty blond waitress, Frankie (Michelle Pfeiffer). But Frankie finds Johnnie too intense and "needy"; she's had too much bad luck with men. Her gay friend and neighbor Tim (Nathan Lane) reminds her that her phone hasn't exactly been ringing off the hook. Agreeing to a date, Frankie is charmed by Johnny but reluctant to get involved in a full-scale relationship. At her apartment one night, the two admire a lovely piece (Debussy's "Clair de Lune") on the radio, and Johnny calls the station to ask them to play it again. Against all odds, the piece is reprised minutes later. Perhaps, the lovers think, their relationship will also work in spite of the odds against it. *Fade out.*

Playing mid-forties at age fifty-one (and getting away with it), Pacino is simply terrific in one of his most delightful pictures. He and Pfeiffer give very realistic

183

Ex-con Johnny asks coffee-shop owner Nick (Hector Elizondo) for a job as Nick's daughter watches.

Al Pacino as Johnny the short-order cook in *Frankie and Johnny*.

depictions of "uncertain" lovers—she, not wanting to offend him but with deep reservations; he, hoping he's charming her but afraid that he's not. Pacino is actually very charming in this picture, whether he's telling another waitress, Cora (Kate Nelligan), why he doesn't cry out or moan during an orgasm or assuring Tim that he, Johnny, has a gay cousin. To Cora, whom he beds, he explains that he was in a place where "full-throated orgasm would have been inappropriate." "Like a monastery?" Cora asks. To Tim, he says of his cousin: "I just found out he was gay a couple of months ago." "I'll look him up in the directory," Tim says wryly. "Under the new listings."

Later, Pacino pulls out the stops when he expresses his full-fledged orgasm with accompanying verbalizations and his joy at having same. Pacino is also wonderful dancing to Greek music with the "stiff" but fun-loving waitress Nedda (Jane Morris) at a party celebrating a busboy's selling his first script to Hollywood. Morris and Pacino seem to be having so much *spontaneous* fun that they make the scene one of the standouts in the picture.

In Terence McNally's stage play *Frankie and Johnny in the Clair de Lune* (Light of the Moon), upon which McNally's screenplay was based, the part of Frankie was essayed by Kathy Bates as an "unattractive, middle-aged woman who had given up on love." The

Johnny is smitten with pretty waitress Frankie (Michelle Pfeiffer) almost from the first.

New York Times said: "The casting of the conspicuously young, exquisitely beautiful, and very bankable Michelle Pfeiffer [in the film] provoked scorn in the theater community."

Yet Pfeiffer—while she may be different from the original conception—is quite good in the picture and has several outstanding scenes. A lonely woman (who is to say pretty women can't be lonely?), she watches other people's lives—among them a woman who is beaten by her husband—through the windows of the building across the street and at one point tries to give herself the Heimlich manuever. Pfeiffer movingly gets through the fear and desperation and loneliness of her character as she tells Johnny about the previous men in her life, including one who fell for her best friend and one who beat her so severely that she miscarried. True, Kathy Bates, plain and overweight, might have been more pathetic in these scenes, but Pfeiffer is no less touching.

Of the rest of the cast, Kate Nelligan is excellent, completely different from her usual self and totally convincing as Cora, the hard-boiled, likable sexpot with whom Johnny dallies for some sexual hijinks. Jane Morris as the slightly weird Nedda is so realistic and irrepressible that one could imagine her being snatched not from central casting but out of some greasy spoon on Broadway. Nathan Lane is delightful as Frankie's confidant Tim, never descending into stereotype, dashing off lines with perfect timing and breezy skill. Sean O'Bryan is also good as Tim's lover, Bobby.

Of the coffee-shop staff, Hector Elizondo is fine, as usual, as Nick, the owner, while Fernando Lopez, Glen Plummer, and Tim Hopper, among others, turn in nice jobs as cooks, busboys, and so on.

McNally's screenplay has only a few false notes, such as when Johnny asks Frankie for a date while they're huddled over an epileptic customer's body

Frankie is fond of Johnny but has deep reservations about dating him.

Frankie's neighbor Tim (Nathan Lane) talks her into dating Johnny and also gives her wardrobe advice.

waiting for an ambulance to arrive. And how does Johnny manage to talk the suspicious, insular Frankie into taking him home to bed on the night of their first date? The two stand talking in front of a truck filled with flowers, but we aren't allowed to hear the dialogue.

Which is a shame, because McNally's dialogue is usually excellent, from the witty gags and trenchant observances to Pacino's explaining to Pfeiffer that he feels like "the only person in the world trapped inside this body, only bumping into people but not connecting with the only other people in the world trapped inside their bodies." In many ways *Frankie and Johnny* is only an updating of all those forties comedies with likable lunatics trying to win over more reserved heroines. Unlike those old films, *Frankie and Johnny* makes good points about smothering, self-centered love.

Some critics felt that the film's ending wrapped things up too neatly. Not only do Frankie and Johnny agree to commit to each other in "the light of the

Johnny tries to chat up Frankie, but she seems to be resisting his charms.

Frankie and Johnny share their first kiss—but not their last.

Frankie shares a laugh at the bowling alley with coworkers Cora (Kate Nelligan, *center*) and Nedda (Jane Morris, *right*).

Frankie and Johnny find themselves falling for each other in spite of the odds.

190

Director Garry Marshall muses over a problem with his two leads.

Hector Elizondo discusses a scene with Al Pacino, Garry Marshall, and Michelle Pfeiffer.

moon," but the battered wife in the next building leaves home the same night. But it is hardly a typical Hollywood happy ending: Frankie and Johnny have only agreed to *try* and make things work, to open themselves to love and all its vulnerabilities and risk heartbreak. Who really knows what will happen in the months ahead? For that matter, who knows what will really happen to the battered wife who has left home?

Garry Marshall's direction is quietly effective and moves things along nicely. Marvin Hamlisch's nice music and funky pop tunes on the soundtrack are pleasant, but of course Debussy's "Clair de Lune" is what really makes the ending work.

Why is Pacino so much better in *Frankie and Johnny* than in his earlier romantic comedy (of sorts) *Author! Author!?* (Not that he was *bad* in the former film.) First there's the fact that McNally's script is far superior to Horovitz's. Second, a naturalistic actor like Pacino is much better playing a real person like Johnny than an unreal *type* like Ivan Trevalian. Besides, as Johnny, he didn't have to strain to be funny; Johnny *is* a man of charm and humor, and Pacino just had to play him that way, not emote in a certain "style."

Frankie and Johnny was a nice change of pace from the "blood and guts" pictures, as would be Pacino's next two films.

GLENGARRY GLEN ROSS

New Line Cinema, 1992

Executive producer, Joseph Caracciolo Jr.; producers, Jerry Tokofsky and Stanley R. Zupnik; director, James Foley; director of photography, Juan Ruiz Anchia; screenplay, David Mamet, based on his play; editor, Howard Smith; music, James Newton Howard; coproducers, Morris Ruskin and Nava Levin; production designer, Jane Musky; costume designer, Jane Greenwood. Running time: 100 min.

CAST

Al Pacino (*Ricky Roma*); Jack Lemmon (*Sheldon Levene*); Alec Baldwin (*Blake*); Ed Harris (*Dave Moss*); Alan Arkin (*George Aaronow*); Kevin Spacey (*John Williamson*); Jonathan Pryce (*James Link*); Bruce Altman (*Mr. Spannel*); Jude Ciccolella (*Detective*).

While it undoubtedly worked even better on the stage, the film adaptation of David Mamet's Pulitzer prize–winning play *Glengarry Glen Ross* is noteworthy if for no other reason than that it gives the audience the opportunity to see several fine actors really putting on a *show*. In particular, Al Pacino, Jack Lemmon, and Ed Harris seem to be in a three-man acting contest, with accompanying pyrotechnics—and these gents *deliver!*

The agents in a real estate firm are told by a slick operator, Blake (Alec Baldwin), from "downtown," that they are, in effect, "fired" and have one week to get their jobs "back." In other words, unless their performances improve, they're through. They must close a deal before the week is up or else. The men complain that they don't have good enough "leads" (names of people to whom they might be able to sell property), and all are hungering for leads to a property in Florida known as the Glengarry Highlands. The manager, John (Kevin Spacey), insists that the Glengarry leads are reserved for those agents who have gotten the best—and most—deals. The likely contender is Ricky Roma (Al Pacino), who has been wining and dining a client, Link (Jonathan Pryce), in a nearby Chinese restaurant.

The most desperate of the group is Shelley Levene (Jack Lemmon), whose daughter's hospital bills have to be paid. John agrees to give the Glengarry leads to Shelley for 25 percent of the commissions and fifty dollars a lead, but Shelley can't come up with the money. Meanwhile, Dave Moss (Ed Harris) and a reluctant George Aaronow (Alan Arkin) plot to steal the leads, which are missing from the office the following morning.

When John lies to Ricky's client, Link (who has

changed his mind), and tells him that his check was cashed and the contract sent downtown, Shelley makes a blunder, telling John that he should never make anything up unless it will be helpful. For once John went home early instead of going downtown with the contracts and demands to know how Shelley knew he was lying. Shelley confesses that *he* stole the leads and sold them to a rival broker. John tells the detective investigating the break-in who the guilty party is; the broken, defeated Shelley will be fired and arrested.

Pacino is very convincing as a somewhat sleazy, oily real estate operator, someone who has developed a certain style but never really had any class. Ricky Roma is more polished than, say, "Scarface" or Pacino's later "Carlito," but only superficially. He's a "cool guy." Pacino looks good, if a little battered, in the role, smooth and urbane.

Glengarry Glen Ross presents mostly fine tuned ensemble acting, but Pacino has several standout moments in the picture, such as when he talks to a nervous Link, trying to placate his fears and convince him not to pull out of the deal. Or when he tells off John for giving him bad leads: "Where did you get this one from—a morgue?" Later, however, Pacino is perhaps too controlled when he gets angry at John for ruining his deal with Link by saying the check has been cashed. "You *never* open your mouth until you

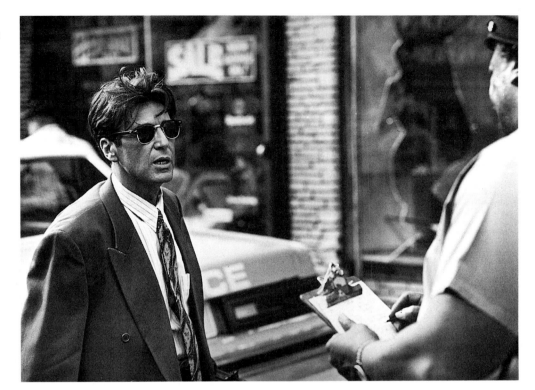

Al Pacino plays real estate agent
Ricky Roma in *Glengarry Glen
Ross*.

know what the shot is!" he screams at the manager. Ricky is properly furious, but Pacino seems too restrained, merely simmering when a real Pacino blast might have been called for. Otherwise, his performance is excellent; he was nominated for an Academy Award, in fact.

Pacino's chief competition is from Jack Lemmon as Shelley Levene. A hypnotically fascinating actor, Lemmon is superb as the tired but still frantically energetic salesman at the end of his rope. Trying to sell property to a potential but disinterested client, Mr. Spannel (Bruce Altman), Lemmon registers charm, grace, hope, defeat, and despair in equal measure. In their best scene together, Lemmon pretends to be another satisfied client so that Pacino can clinch the deal with the almost hysterical Link. The two men, such different types of actors, clearly play well together and are having fun. These are two thespian powerhouses at their peak.

Ed Harris is also dynamic as Dave Moss, tough, macho, but essentially a complaining loser. Harris manages to make a man who would probably not be very interesting in real life seem fascinating, subtly revealing the weakness beneath the strong, masculine exterior. Alec Baldwin really makes the most of his one scene as Blake from "downtown" who threatens

195

"What, me worry?" Ricky seems to say,
but he doesn't know his latest client
wants out of the deal.

196

Pacino checks a point with the director of *Glengarry Glen Ross*.

197

everyone with dismissal. Baldwin took a risk in playing it in a more stylized, slick manner than the others' naturalistic emoting, but it pays off in the long run: His Blake emerges as menacing, powerful, larger-than-life loathsome, almost a force of nature, all the conscienceless "winners" in the world combined into one obscene, smirking *presence.*

Although their roles are less "showy," the other actors also score, particularly Kevin Spacey as the manager, John, and Jonathan Pryce (with a convincing American accent) as James Link, Ricky's client. Both actors have been powerhouses in other roles, but here they underplay, slowly building up to their bigger scenes: Pryce, weak but determined, walking away from the deal with Ricky; Spacey telling Shelley that he basically set him up because he just doesn't like him. Alan Arkin as quiet George, Bruce Altman as Mr. Spannel, and Jude Ciccolella as the detective are also just right.

Glengarry Glen Ross is not exactly *Death of a Salesman,* but it is absorbing and occasionally powerful. The opening scenes, with all their tedious, confusing real estate chatter, hardly draw one in, but the movie eventually builds in tension and interest. The story line is basically old-fashioned; as in Rod Serling's *Patterns,* we're handed the creepy boss who wants his employees to improve business or *leave.* The picture is well edited by Howard Smith and briskly directed by James Foley. The jazz rifts James Newton Howard composed for the score are forgettable, however.

Ricky's confidence begins to crumble when he realizes his client has backed out.

SCENT OF A WOMAN

Universal; a City Light Films production, 1992

Executive producer, Ronald L. Schwary; producer, Martin Brest; director, Brest; director of photography, Donald E. Thorn; screenplay, Bo Goldman; editors, William Steinkamp, Michael Tronick, and Harvey Rosenstock; music, Thomas Newman; production designer, Angelo Graham; costume designer, Aude Bronson-Howard. Running time: 137 min.

CAST

Al Pacino (*Frank Slade*); Chris O'Donnell (*Charlie Sims*); James Rebhorn (*Trask*); Philip S. Hoffman (*George Willis Jr.*); Nicholas Sadler (*Harry Havemeyer*); Richard Venture (*W. R. Slade*); Bradley Whitford (*Randy*); Margaret Eginton (*Gail*); Rochelle Oliver (*Gretchen*); Tom Riis Farrell (*Garry*); Gabrielle Anwar (*Donna*); Leonard Gaines (*Freddie Bisco*); Ron Eldard (*Officer Gore*).

By 1992, Al Pacino had received Academy Award nominations for Best Actor or Best Supporting Actor for, among others, such pictures as *Serpico, Dog Day Afternoon,* and *. . . and Justice for All.* What an irony that he should finally *win* the Best Actor Oscar for *Scent of a Woman*!

Certainly Pacino gives a fine performance in the film as retired colonel Frank Slade, a charming, blind reprobate obsessed with "pussy" and suicide. But the part could hardly have been tailor-made for the miscast Pacino (he triumphs over the miscasting, however). As written, Frank Slade is more of a role for Charles Durning or even the older (than Pacino), grizzled Ben Gazzara. Played by Pacino—however winningly—Frank Slade never seems quite like a real person. But then Bo Goldman's script does little to make the colonel seem real to begin with.

Charlie Sims (Chris O'Donnell) is a student at the Baird prep school in New Hampshire. For extra money, he agrees to "baby-sit" for the disagreeable and vulgar Frank Slade, a blind middle-aged man who lives with his niece and husband, while they go on vacation. Charlie expects this to be an easy—if unpleasant—assignment, but Slade surprises him by insisting he accompany him to New York City. After Slade has a good meal at the Oak Room, dances a tango with a sexy restaurant patron, and sleeps with a high-class call girl, he attempts suicide in his hotel room. Charlie prevents him from blowing his brains out. "Why shouldn't I kill myself?" asks Slade, who is ready to exit after his final fling. "Because you can dance a tango and drive a Ferrari better than anyone I've ever seen," says Charlie (typical of the picture's often puerile dialogue).

The two return to New Hampshire, where further

The blind colonel dances a tango with Donna (Gabrielle Anwar), whom he meets in a restaurant.

Frank and Charlie pose
with the red Ferrari.

201

Al Pacino as retired colonel Frank Slade in *Scent of a Woman*.

adventure awaits. It seems that Charlie knows who participated in a practical joke on the headmaster, Trask (James Rebhorn), and is threatened with expulsion unless he reveals their identities. The headmaster practically guarantees his entry into a superior university if he does snitch. At a public hearing over the matter, who should advance up to the stage but Frank Slade, who argues in Charlie's favor and commends his integrity. "He won't sell anybody out to buy his future." The students applaud Slade, and the board votes not to expel Charlie. *Finis*.

Frank Slade is an utterly self-centered person—at times, he seems pathetic; at others, a borderline psycho—but as played by Pacino, he slowly begins to

Frank and Charlie Sims (Chris O'Donnell), his human "guide dog," set off for New York.

grow on you . . . to a point. As has often been the case in his career, Pacino's personal charm makes an unpleasant character more bearable. Conversely, it is also possible that Pacino tries *too* hard not to sentimentalize the colonel. Pacino's jivey, vaguely southern accent that comes and goes also seems a little "odd."

Chris O'Donnell is okay as the shy, shuffling Charlie, with his hangdog look, but he doesn't seem nearly nervous enough at the climactic hearing. It is hard to imagine the very shy Charlie able to lead Pacino over to a strange beauty in a restaurant (without at least having had a beer or two first) and being so at ease. A budding bleeding heart, Charlie tells Slade, "You're not bad; you're just in pain." Slade's words of wisdom for Charlie: "There are only two syllables in this whole wide world worth hearing: pussy." (To his cat Slade opines: "When in doubt, fuck.")

A tense Thanksgiving dinner scene—Slade just shows up at his brother's house, uninvited, with Char-

Slade argues Charlie's case at the hearing.

lie in tow—is one of the best segments in the movie, illustrating the dual nature of Slade's personality. On the one hand, he is admirably frank and earthy, fun-loving. On the other hand, he can be overbearingly obnoxious. His relatives are undeniably "uptight," but Slade goes too far. His nephew Randy (Bradley Whitford) declares: "He was an asshole before; now he's a blind asshole."

Slade *is* an asshole and in many ways unsympathetic. He lost his eyesight during a grenade-juggling

contest when he was drunk! While in New York with Charlie, he convinces a dealer to let them take a Ferrari out for a spin and speeds along the streets in it, not caring what happens to himself, young Charlie, or any pedestrians. The scene is supposed to be "cute"; instead (like so many scenes in this picture) it's irritating.

A "drama" for the sitcom generation, *Scent of a Woman* is as phony and contrived as a bad made-for-television movie. Far too many scenes are put in for confrontation value but have no real point to them. The headmaster, Trask, is supposed to be such a villain, but we are told more about him than we are *shown*. Considering the humiliating joke played on him (a big balloon filled with paint poured over his new car and him before the assembled students), his determination to get the pranksters seems more than reasonable.

But the picture really implodes at the climactic hearing and as the result of Pacino's big speech, which is embarrassingly overdone. "If it were five years ago," he says, "I'd take a flamethrower to this place!" The students applaud Pacino, but in real life they would probably find him laughable.

And what about the hearing? Certainly Charlie has been placed in an extremely difficult position by the headmaster, who *is* being unfair. But what about the students who actually perpetrated the practical joke (or, more accurately, the mean-spirited act of vandalism)? What about *their* integrity? They sit smirking in the audience, perfectly willing to let Charlie be expelled for his silence, absolutely *un*willing to take responsibility for their actions.

It never occurs to anyone connected with *Scent of a Woman* that its message of so-called integrity is patently phony. Why should Charlie throw away his future for "friends" (with friends like these . . .) who are willing, if not anxious, to let him take the fall, who don't have the guts to come forward, admit their complicity, and let Charlie off the hook? By not getting Charlie out of trouble, regardless of the consequences (they *did* commit the deed, after all), they prove their unworthiness. Charlie *should* have turned them in once he realized they were *not* going to do the right thing.

At 137 minutes, *Scent of a Woman* is much too long, and Martin Brest's direction (along with three editors) isn't able to prevent tedium from setting in long before the conclusion. Some of the supporting cast certainly do their best to help pep things up: Richard Venture expertly limns the affectionate exasperation he feels for Slade as his brother; Bradley Whitford is fine as the not so affectionate nephew; James Rebhorn is solid as headmaster Trask; and Leonard Gaines makes the most of his bit as Freddie Bisco, the Ferrari dealer who is so reluctant to let Slade and Charlie take one of his cars out for a spin. Gabrielle Anwar got some press as Donna, the lady with whom Slade dances the tango; she has little to do in the film but does it well.

The ex-officer and the young gentleman arrive in the big city.

The colonel stands up for his young friend Charlie at the prep-school hearing.

Ditto for Ron Eldard as a handsome cop who fails to notice that Pacino is blind when he pulls up to the Ferrari. The college students and assorted relatives of Slade are also well cast.

Donald E. Thorn's photography is excellent and crisp, making the most of great-looking New York City locations, not to mention New England. Thomas Newman's theme music, with its lively bells and guitars, is irresistible.

One reason Pacino may have done the picture is to accept the challenge of playing a blind person, a challenge he is more than up to. You never question that Frank Slade is without sight; Pacino *is* blind, or seems to be. He plays a "visually impaired" person so naturally that it never seems like a stunt. Undoubtedly, it had much to do with his winning the Oscar. *Scent of Woman* was also nominated for Best Director and Best Screenplay, as well as Best Picture; only Pacino won.

Scent of a Woman was based on the 1974 Italian film *Profumo di Donna.*

CARLITO'S WAY

Universal/Epic Productions, 1993

Executive producers, Louis A. Stroller and Ortwin Frey-ermuth; producers, Martin Bregman, Willi Baer, and Michael S. Bregman; director, Brian De Palma; director of photography, Stephen H. Burum; screenplay, David Koepp; based on the novels *Carlito's Way* and *After Hours* by Edwin Torres; editors, Bill Pankow and Kristina Boden; music, Patrick Doyle; production designer, Richard Sylbert; costume designer, Aude Bronson-Howard. Running time: 145 min.

CAST

Al Pacino (*Carlito Brigante*); Sean Penn (*David Kleinfeld*); Penelope Ann Miller (*Gail*); John Leguizamo (*Benny Blanco*); Ingrid Rogers (*Steffie*); Luis Guzmán (*Pachonga*); James Rebhorn (*Norwalk*); Joseph Sirayo (*Vinnie Taglialucca*); Frank Minucci (*Tony Taglialucca*); Viggo Mortensen (*Lilon*); Jorge Porcel (*Saso*); Adrian Pasona (*Frankie*).

It was back to the world of sleaze and drugs and nefarious characters for Pacino and director Brian De Palma, who had previously teamed for *Scarface.*

In New York City's court of appeals in 1975, the judge heartily lambastes the district attorney's "unfortunate investigative techniques" that are allowing

Al Pacino as ex-con Carlito Brigante in *Carlito's Way.*

criminal Carlito Brigante (Pacino) to go free after serving only five years of his thirty-year sentence. Brigante has had enough of jail and tells everyone that he intends to go straight. Back in his neighborhood, a crony, Pachonga (Luis Guzmán) bemoans how things have changed, how the kids in the game refuse to play by the rules and are much more violent.

Halfheartedly, Carlito accompanies his young cousin, who is a delivery boy in a drug deal, and gets firsthand knowledge of the ugly new world he is now living in. The dealers murder his cousin and try to kill him, but he fights back successfully, absconding with $30,000 that no one is left to claim. He uses the money

Carlito checks out the old neighborhood with his buddies.

to buy an interest in a disco; as soon as he has saved up $75,000, he intends to head for Florida and open a legitimate car dealership.

But the fates seem to conspire against Carlito. His lawyer, David Kleinfeld (Sean Penn), has been told by a tough client to help spring him from Riker's Island *or else* and enlists a grateful but reluctant Carlito in the scheme. Carlito is stunned when Kleinfeld murders both the client and his son because the lawyer kept a million-dollar payoff he was supposed to forward to another party. Soon both the police and the client's other son are hunting Carlito; Kleinfeld betrays him to the D.A. to save his own skin; his business

partner in the disco tries to appropriate all his savings; and his buddy Pachonga also turns traitor. Carlito manages to outwit his many pursuers and make it to Grand Central Station, but he's shot to death by a punk and would-be kingpin he once insulted just as he is about to board a train to Florida with his girlfriend. (Some days you just can't win.)

Although it is questionable whether his acting could really be described as "great," Pacino swaggers through *Carlito's Way* with all his star charisma intact. He is sensational as Carlito, registering force and dynamism in every scene. He looks great in a beard and a seventies hairstyle, although the Hispanic accent he "wears" sort of comes and goes. Pacino gives a ludicrous character much more dignity than he deserves.

Carlito wants to go straight, but practically from the first he must resort to violence to defend himself.

Sean Penn proves again that he is one of our greatest young actors with his performance as mob lawyer David Kleinfeld. Penn never lays all his cards on the table; he never telegraphs his character's actions (which some actors do regardless of the script). There's no clue that nerdy Kleinfeld can be as brutal as the gangsters he represents, that he can be sexually aggressive and viciously underhanded. Penn unveils each loathsome layer with great skill and authority and is totally convincing every step of the way.

Penelope Ann Miller, as the dancer, Gail, with whom Carlito renews his relationship, is a bit too glossy and superficial in the part, not exhibiting the surface hardness that such a woman would have to have to be in love with a man in Carlito's profession. (To be fair, the character is unconvincing to begin with.) Miller does have a hot love scene with Pacino, with whom she had a brief liaison during filming. (De Palma's revolving camera during this sequence is yet another variation of the Jimmy Stewart–Kim Novak kiss in Hitchcock's *Vertigo,* but at least it is more effective than the one in De Palma's *Body Double.*) Ingrid Rogers certainly scores as the sexy, brazen disco dancer, Steffie, who eventually becomes Kleinfeld's lover.

James Rebhorn (D.A. Norwalk) was a brief adversary of Pacino's as the headmaster in *Scent of a Woman;* here he's really out to get him and plays each scene with his customary verisimilitude. Frank Minucci registers so much menace as the dreaded Tony Taglialucca, the incarcerated client of Kleinfeld's who was cheated out of a million by his own lawyer, that he's one of the best—and most frightening—things in the picture. John Leguizamo hits the mark as Benny Blanco, the punk who kills Carlito, and Luis Guzmán is also notable as Carlito's crony Pachonga. Also good are Jorge Porcel as Carlito's disco partner, Saso, and Joseph Sirayo and Adrian Pasona as Tony Taglialucca's sons, Vinnie and Frankie.

An actor who deserves special mention is Viggo Mortensen, as Lilon, a hood who has been condemned to life in a wheelchair and wears a wire to a meeting with Carlito. When Carlito learns of his duplicity, Lilon breaks down into blubbering begging and self-pity. Mortensen manages to make you feel sorry for someone who doesn't deserve much sympathy and plays with such strength and conviction that he positively steals the scene from Pacino.

Although, like *Scarface, Carlito's Way* doesn't have much of the famous camera trickery De Palma employs in his shockers, there are several outstanding scenes. Among them is the tense sequence when Carlito accompanies his cousin to the den of the drug

Carlito entertains his girlfriend Gail (Penelope Ann Miller) and his lawyer at his disco.

Carlito confers with his hotshot criminal lawyer David Kleinfeld (Sean Penn).

An intoxicated Kleinfeld listens to Carlito's counsel.

dealers behind the barbershop. There's a game of pool going on. The friendly head of the drug gang wants Carlito's cousin to bend down and get a soda out of a large ice chest by the wall.

Somebody goes to the bathroom. Everything seems absolutely normal, and yet something's *not quite right*. De Palma milks the scene for so much suspense that it is almost a relief when the dealers show their true colors and the violence finally begins.

Also outstanding is the sequence involving Kleinfeld and Carlito's alleged "rescue" of gangster Taglialucca from the river after he manages to escape from

the Riker's prison barge. Pretending to offer Taglialucca a helping hand up into the boat, Kleinfeld instead bashes his brains in and lets him drown. He also murders one of his sons who is on board before Carlito can stop him. The only misstep occurs early in this scene when a nervous Kleinfeld is preparing to set sail with Carlito, who doesn't really want to be a part of it but feels he has a debt to pay. "Untie the fuckin' rope, you spick!" screams Kleinfeld. While Carlito may not be the mad dog Tony Montana of *Scarface*, it's unlikely that he would let such a slur go by without comment, especially when you consider that he'd rather be anywhere else at that moment.

The film's lengthy chase climax, which begins at the disco and culminates at Grand Central, is also memorable. First there's a suspenseful bit with Carlito attempting to get his savings from a hiding place without Taglialucca's surviving son—who wants both him and Kleinfeld *dead*—seeing him retrieve it *and* to leave the club. Then there's a protracted sequence when Carlito tries to elude his pursuers in the subway. Finally, the shootout in Grand Central, where Carlito disposes of the gang that's after him but falls victim to the inimitable Benny Blanco just when he thinks he's home safe. The whole trip is very exciting, but the bit with Pacino lying down horizontally on the escalator to the Graybar Building to avoid detection is a bit much.

Carlito just wants to live happily ever after with his woman, but fate has other plans for the couple.

A quieter but equally intense scene has Carlito checking up on his lady love, Gail, whom he has not seen for five years, as she dances in a studio to the strains of Delibes's *Lakmé*. Carlito, thinking he has lost her forever, watches from outside in the pouring rain with only a garbage-can lid for cover.

David Koepp's screenplay certainly keeps things percolating, and De Palma never fails to bring to vivid life all the twists and turns of the story. Stephen H. Burum's cinematography sharply illuminates the New York City locations, such as the village, uptown, and a very early morning (or expert re-creation of) Grand Central Station. Patrick Doyle's music adds tautness to the subway chase and other scenes. However, it is a little overdone at the end when Carlito dies, trying to summon up a sense of inappropriate pathos; Carlito is hardly some tragic hero, after all.

Like *Scarface*, *Carlito's Way*, with its world of dealers and losers, is enormously entertaining. Also like *Scarface*, it pretty much avoids dealing with the morality of it all. *Carlito's Way* is a good B movie but nothing more.

Carlito doesn't show punk Benny Blanco (John Leguizano) any respect, and he pays for it in the end.

Carlito and henchman ponder whether or not to kill Benny Blanco.

213

CITY HALL

Castle Rock Films, 1995

Director, Harold Becker; screenplay, Ken Lipper and Bo Goldman.

CAST

Al Pacino (*the Mayor*); John Cusack (*Deputy Mayor*); Bridget Fonda (*Investigator*).

Al Pacino started shooting *City Hall* in New York City in October 1994. In this he plays the ultimate New Yorker: His Honor, the mayor. The script was written by Ken Lipper (and polished by *Scent of a Woman* writer Bo Goldman), who was deputy mayor under Ed Koch. Lipper previously wrote the screenplay for *Wall Street,* starring Michael Douglas.

The story deals with a medical technician at the Metropolitan Hospital in Harlem whose child is mur-dered. He determines to discover the truth but comes up against a wall of bureaucracy. Powerful New York politicians, such as the mayor (Pacino) and his deputy mayor (John Cusack), find themselves caught up in an investigation launched by Bridget Fonda.

Harold Becker, who directed *Sea of Love* with Pacino, was at the helm. As was the case with several previous Pacino pictures, many New York locations were featured in the movie.

PART THREE
HIS PLAYS

Portrait of Al Pacino as a young, hopeful actor in New York City.

Scoring a triumph on (a return to) Broadway as Herod in the Lincoln Center production of Wilde's *Salome*. English actress Susan Bertish plays Herodias.

Al Pacino's dedication to the art of acting is proven by his continued interest in a variety of theatrical ventures, all of which pay far less than his movie roles and many of which could be considered highly "risky." But it was in the theatrical circles of New York, where he was born, that he first made his mark. And he goes back to his "roots" on a periodic basis.

Pacino's earliest roles were in children's theater pieces at such places as the Cafe Bizarre and Theater East in New York. Later on, he was associated with Cafe La Mama—where he tried stand-up comedy—and the Living Theater, where he worked as a stagehand with Martin Sheen. Pacino had to do other kinds of part-time work to survive during this period.

His acting coach at Herbert Berghof's studios, Charlie Laughton, had his class do a reading of William Saroyan's *Hello, Out There.* Laughton was acquainted with Joe Cino of the Caffe Cino and asked him to sit in on one of the readings. Cino was impressed enough to offer to stage the show at his cafe, leading to Pacino's off-Broadway debut. For the first time he was acting in front of a paying audience.

Hello, Out There was followed by Strindberg's *Creditors,* which Charlie Laughton mounted for a song in Lower Manhattan. Sometimes the actors onstage out-

numbered the customers in the audience. Despite the lack of attendance—or maybe because of it—Pacino was able to overcome his jitters and a feeling of inadequacy and emerged as top contender for acting honors in the production.

By 1966 he was in the full bloom of confidence, bolstered by encouragement from Laughton and his peers, and proved particularly impressive in Fred Vassi's *Why Is a Crooked Letter.* Although performed in yet another of New York's seemingly inexhaustible supply of shoestring off-Broadway companies—Alec Rubin's Theater of Encounter on West Seventy-second Street—the play did garner Pacino a lot of attention *and* a nomination for an Obie, the awards given for off- and off-off-Broadway productions.

In the 1960s he also appeared with black powerhouse James Earl Jones in a production of John Wolfson's *Peace Creeps* at the New Theater Workshop. By this time he had been accepted at the prestigious Actors Studio and been befriended by the studio's head and top acting coach Lee Strasberg, who gave his new student both tea and sympathy and a great deal of encouragement. Pacino made up his mind that he would only accept worthy parts and not just take an assignment for the money. While his integrity

217

could not be questioned, this often meant he went hungry when he didn't have to.

For instance, in 1966 he traveled to Massachusetts to meet with David Wheeler, head of the prestigious Theater Company of Boston, whose company he wished to join. According to Pacino's biographer Andrew Yule, Wheeler offered Pacino fifty dollars a week (no mean sum for an actor in those days), but the part in the company's first production was too "small" to suit Pacino, and he turned Wheeler down despite the fact that later productions might have garnered him more substantial roles. Pacino had to borrow money from Wheeler to get a bus back to New York.

A year later, Pacino did temporarily join the company, appearing in two productions at the Charles Playhouse: Clifford Odets's *Awake and Sing!* and Jean-Claude Van Itallie's *America, Hurrah.* It was in the latter production that Pacino worked with Jill Clayburgh, who became his live-in lover for several years before marrying playwright David Rabe and becoming a (limited) star (of *An Unmarried Woman* and other films) in her own right.

Pacino really began to "make it" with his next role, that of street punk and sociopath Murph in Israel Horovitz's *The Indian Wants the Bronx.* He had appeared in a workshop production of the play in Connecticut in 1966, but this new production was fully mounted for New York's Astor Place Theater. Pacino costarred with Matthew Cowles and John Cazale, with whom he had a close friendship until Cazale's death from cancer.

The Indian Wants the Bronx deals with two tough guys who come across an elderly Indian gentleman while wandering about Manhattan one night. They tease and torment the man, who only wants to get out to the Bronx to visit a relative. The Indian man is eventually beaten and finally stabbed. Much of the action revolves around a phone booth, which almost functions as a fourth character, a would-be lifeline for the abused Indian man. During the play Pacino strutted about in a menacing manner, shouting out, "Hey, pussyface!" to a woman in a window, using his swagger to disguise the basic insecurity of Murph the malicious. It won him a Best Actor Obie and established him as an actor to be reckoned with from that day forward. John Cazale and Israel Horovitz also won Obies.

A disturbing play in the sixties, Horovitz's study of xenophobia and restless youth undoubtedly would seem quaint and dated in these days of metal protectors in grade schools, its Murph an all-too-typical nihilistic, marauding moron of the nineties.

Pacino followed up this triumph with Don Petersen's *Does a Tiger Wear a Necktie?* in 1969, his Broadway debut at the Belasco Theatre. This study of the inner workings of a drug halfway house garnered Pacino even more attention—he made his film debut in *Me, Natalie* that same year—but it had a short run, and many felt Pacino's role of sadistic whacko "Bickham," as well as other roles to come, was too similar to his Murph. One critic praised Pacino's "ceaseless soft treadmill stance, sniffing nose and blinking eyes, the fingers that constantly scrabble at the air as if scratching the invisible monkey on his back. . . ." Pacino was awarded a Best Supporting Actor Tony for his performance. That fine actor Hal Holbrook was also in the cast.

Pacino was sorely disappointed with the results when he next appeared in a production of Heathcote Williams's *The Local Stigmatic* at the Actors Playhouse in 1969. On the same bill were several Harold Pinter plays, but these weren't enough to bring in the paying customers. *The Local Stigmatic* would have closed on opening night, except that John Voight (costar of Dustin Hoffman in *Midnight Cowboy*), who wasn't even in the cast, used his own funds to keep it running a week longer.

Many dismissed *The Local Stigmatic* as a clone of *The Indian Wants the Bronx.* Again Pacino was cast as a sociopathic loser who terrorizes an elderly man with the help of a buddy. Pacino has always been intrigued by the play, for in it the victim is a famous actor and the two punks destroy him out of jealousy of his achievements. Pacino was just getting a taste of fame in 1969 but was a major movie star by 1976 when Joseph Papp restaged *The Local Stigmatic* for a "by invitation only" audience at his Public Theater. By this time Pacino knew firsthand about fame and people who were jealous of your achievements, who hated you because of your press clippings. So fascinated was he by *The Local Stigmatic* that he put his own money in a still-uncompleted short film version of Williams's unsuccessful play.

Pacino's next theatrical venture was a revival of Tennessee Williams's *Camino Real* for the Lincoln Center Repertory Theater. A lesser but still interesting play by the author of *Cat on a Hot Tin Roof, Vieux Carré,* and other masterpieces, *Camino Real* has more than its share of heart-wrenching, powerful sequences, most of which were undermined by Milton Katselas's direction, which tried to turn the play into a campy comedy. Pacino, who made his entrance swinging over the audience and dropping onto the stage, survived this version unscathed, however, and even the great playwright was happily purring at "Kilroy's" energy onstage. Pacino got mostly good notices, but some felt there was a numbing sameness to his performances that he had better snap out of or else.

Also in 1970, Pacino returned to David Wheeler's company in Boston, this time to *direct* a new Israel Horovitz play entitled *Rats*. The play never amounted to much, and Pacino hasn't directed since, but he did strike up a long-term association with Wheeler's artistic troupe. For the next ten years, during which his film career flourished, all of his major theatrical appearances were with Wheeler's company.

First there was David Rabe's *Basic Training of Pavlo Hummel*, which had already played at Joseph Papp's Public Theater without Pacino. Part of Rabe's Vietnam trilogy, which included *Streamers* and *Sticks and Bones*, the play dealt with draftees and how they coped with being stuck in the army during an unpopular war. Pacino's title character was a goofball who slowly matures during the stage play's running time. Many of the actors Pacino worked with in this revival would later turn up in supporting roles in his movies when *The Godfather* turned him into a star that same year. This wasn't just kindness on Pacino's part; rarely did he work with untalented people.

Wheeler took the revival of *The Basic Training of Pavlo Hummel* to Broadway five years later, when Pacino was famous. It had a more than respectful run at the Longacre Theatre, and Pacino won a Best Actor Tony for his performance. Notices were mixed, but generally favorable, in no small part due to the fact that critics, through his movies, could see how wide a range Pacino had. One critic noted that Pacino could essay the smooth, urbane Michael Corleone and the misfit-nitwit Pavlo Hummel with equal skill and veracity.

Another Wheeler production that moved from Boston to Broadway was *Richard III,* in which Pacino's portrayal of the title role was, to put it mildly, controversial. From the first he was lambasted for his audacity as much as he was coddled for his courage. How *dare* this Bronx-by-way-of-Manhattan boy with his appalling New Yorkese enact the bard as if he'd come

An early success in the David Rabe play *The Basic Training of Pavlo Hummel.*

direct from Stratford-on-Avon, naysayers seemed to crow. Others felt that Pacino should be given credit for choosing such a noncommercial play and challenging role. The reviews were mostly brutal, but in the din a few encouraging voices were heard. (The same thing happened when Pacino attempted a period piece for the movies, *Revolution.*)

219

The general consensus was that Pacino was using his Hollywood clout to muscle in on territory better left to Shakespearean specialists and the British and that he tried to win the audience to his side by making the bloody story of *Richard III* seem little different from the saga of the Corleone family. The UPI lively-arts editor was merciless: "He is a Richard who winks and leers at the audience and addresses his soliloquies to it, who spits out every word as if he hated the English language, who gives no indication what makes him tick, who plays for cheap laughs, and whose manner would never fool his royal brother or anyone else into believing a word he says. . . . All I can imagine is that movie star Pacino, who claims a cult following in the 18-to-25 age bracket, is playing for that young audience, trying to recreate the first production back in about 1692, giving the 'groundlings' a few extra laughs."

On the other hand, *Time* magazine declared: "[Pacino's] Richard may be a monster, yet how heroic and finally touching a monster Pacino makes him." Indeed, many felt Pacino's performance was quite passionate, energetic, and thoroughly superior but that most critics couldn't see past the (admittedly inappropriate) New York accent, unfortunate pronunciations, and certain ill-advised aspects of the production, such as costumes that mixed "the medieval with the modern." His habit of frequently spitting as he unleashed his dialogue didn't endear him to the critics, either. "He spits *all the time* on stage," says celebrity watcher and *Hollywood Royalty* author Gregory Speck. "If you sit in the front row you'd need an umbrella!"

Richard III was followed by Bertolt Brecht's *Resistible Rise of Arturo Ui,* which Wheeler staged at the Charles Playhouse in Boston. Paralleling the events in Nazi Germany, the play presented its title gangster as a grotesque Hitlerian figure. Both Pacino and the production got mixed reviews. Joseph Papp had originally underwritten the production with an eye to bringing it to New York, but assorted strains with Pacino and a basic lack of faith in the overall product prevented it from happening.

Pacino's next project was David Mamet's *American Buffalo,* in 1980, which he took from New Haven to New York (a successful five-month run) to Washington, D.C., at the Kennedy Center, and finally to the Duke of York Theatre in London. The play had debuted five years earlier with a different cast at New

York's Theater at St. Clement's Church, of which Pacino was an ardent supporter, then made its way to another off-Broadway theater and finally to Broadway. Pacino's revival began life in New Haven at the Long Wharf Theater.

In the play Pacino is once again cast as a psychotic, but this one spends his time plotting to steal a rare coin instead of pummeling elderly actors or Indians. By the time Pacino got ahold of it, *American Buffalo* had been transformed from a straight drama to a kind of burlesque, with playwright Mamet nodding his approval over both versions. Pacino's off-Broadway rendition at the Downtown Circle in the Square was a smash hit, necessitating a move uptown to the Booth Theatre on Broadway. Pacino was devastated when early in the run his young costar Jimmy Hayden died of a drug overdose; he had been playing a junkie. Although the play itself got mixed notices, Pacino's reviews were generally raves. A few critics suggested that Pacino was technically proficient but too "surfacy."

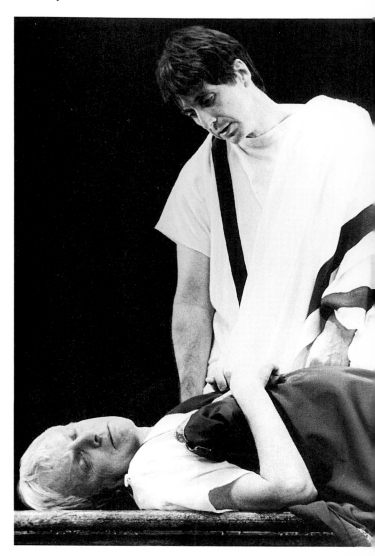

With John McMartin in the Joseph Papp production of *Julius Caesar* at the Public/Newman Theater.

Pacino's next project came along almost accidentally. Pacino had just shown his film version of *The Local Stigmatic* to Joseph Papp, who had produced one version of the play at his Public Theater. Papp, who also produced the New York Shakespeare Festival, asked Pacino which role, above all others, he would like to essay. "We were in the elevator here," Papp told the *New York Post*'s Diana Maychick, "and without missing a beat, Al said, 'Marc Antony.' And I just said, 'You got the part.'" Stuart Vaughan directed the production of *Julius Caesar* for Papp's Public Theater in 1988. Pacino shared the stage with Ed Herrmann and old buddy and former roommate Martin Sheen.

In 1992, Pacino appeared in a double bill at the Circle in the Square in New York. In Oscar Wilde's *Salome*, he played Herod to Sheryl Lee's Salome. In Ira Lewis's *Chinese Coffee* he was one half of a photographer-writer team that was down on its luck. According to *Variety*, the double bill was "a season extra, added as a benefit with a $50 ticket. Pacino missed several performances and cut back the schedule to seven shows a week. So instead of benefiting, Circle in the Square barely broke even."

Over the years Pacino had also been involved with assorted staged readings, workshop productions, and aborted projects that were never seen by the general public. These include Bertolt Brecht's *Jungle of the Cities*, Shakespeare's *Hamlet*, Phil Young's *Crystal Clear*, and Dennis McIntyre's *National Anthem*. Such plays as *Othello* and *The Hairy Ape* never made it out of rehearsal.

LIST OF MAJOR STAGE APPEARANCES

1963: *Hello, Out There*, William Saroyan. Caffe Cino, New York.

1965: *The Creditors*, August Strindberg. The Actors' Gallery, New York.

1966: *Why Is a Crooked Letter*, Fred Vassi. Theater of Encounter, New York (Obie nomination).

1966: *The Indian Wants the Bronx*, Israel Horovitz. Eugene O'Neill Memorial Theater, Connecticut.

1966: *The Peace Creeps*, John Wolfson. New Theater Workshop, New York.

1967: *Awake and Sing!*, Clifford Odets. Charles Playhouse, Boston.

1967: *America, Hurrah*, Jean-Claude Van Itallie. Charles Playhouse, Boston.

1968: *The Indian Wants the Bronx*, Israel Horovitz. Astor Place Theater, New York (Best Actor, Obie).

1969: *Does a Tiger Wear a Necktie?*, Don Petersen. Belasco Theatre. New York (Best Dramatic Supporting Actor, Tony).

1969: *The Local Stigmatic*, Heathcote Williams. Actors Playhouse, New York.

1970: *Camino Real*, Tennessee Williams. Lincoln Center Repertory Theater, New York.

1972: *The Basic Training of Pavlo Hummel*, David Rabe. Charles Theater, Boston.

1972: *Richard III*, William Shakespeare. Loeb Drama Center, Boston.

1975: *The Resistible Rise of Arturo Ui*, Bertolt Brecht. Charles Playhouse, Boston.

1976: *The Local Stigmatic*, Heathcote Williams. Public Theater, New York.

1977: *The Basic Training of Pavlo Hummel*, David Rabe. Longacre Theatre, New York (Best Dramatic Actor, Tony).

1979: *Richard III*, William Shakespeare. Cort Theatre, New York.

1980: *American Buffalo*, David Mamet. Long Wharf Theater Company, New Haven.

1982: *American Buffalo*, David Mamet. Downtown Circle in the Square, New York.

1983: *American Buffalo*, David Mamet. Booth Theatre, New York.

1988: *Julius Caesar*, William Shakespeare. New York Shakespeare Festival Theater, New York.

1992: *Salome*, Oscar Wilde. *Chinese Coffee*, Ira Lewis. Circle in the Square, New York.

BIBLIOGRAPHY

BOOKS

Bouzereau, Laurent. *The DePalma Cut.* New York: Dembner Books, 1988.

Cross, Milton. *Complete Stories of the Great Operas.* New York: Doubleday, 1955.

Quirk, Lawrence J. *Margaret Sullavan: Child of Fate.* New York: St. Martin's Press, 1986.

————. *The Films of Warren Beatty.* New York: Citadel Press, 1990.

————. *The Great War Films.* New York: Citadel Press, 1994.

Schoell, William. *Stay Out of the Shower: 25 Years of Shocker Films Beginning with "Psycho."* New York: Dembner Books, 1985.

Yule, Andrew. *Al Pacino: A Life on the Wire.* New York: Donald I. Fine, 1991.

PERIODICALS

New York Post, New York Daily News, Variety, New York Times, Quirk's Reviews, GQ.

ABOUT THE AUTHOR

Like Al Pacino, William Schoell (rhymes with bowl) is a native New Yorker and once starred as "Murph" in *The Indian Wants the Bronx*—but only in a college production. Happily devoid of any acting ambitions, Mr. Schoell instead turned his attentions to the field of writing. Before publishing his first book in 1984, Schoell worked for Columbia Pictures, for a major New York City law firm, and was even a Manhattan radio talk-show host. A full-time writer, he has authored such novels as *Fatal Beauty, The Pact, Late at Night,* and *The Dragon* as well as several books on film, popular culture, and celebrities. His articles and stories have appeared in numerous national periodicals. Each December in New York, along with film historian Lawrence J. Quirk, he tenders the prestigious James R. Quirk Awards to noteworthy individuals in the motion-picture business and related pursuits.